BEN SMITH

Minimalism

Contents

Introduction

I want to thank you and congratulate you for downloading the book, "Minimalism: How to Simplify and Declutter Your Life With Minimalist Habits."

This book contains proven steps and strategies on deliberately settling for less in order to gain more out of your life and live it the way you want to.

Like many people, you likely have too many possessions that they have become a veritable source of clutter and a heavy burden to bear, what with all the cleaning and organizing that comes with owning them. Your big home may be filled to the brim with all of the fancy stuff that your heart could yearn for — but guess what? You still aren't happy. In fact, you have this void inside you that you fear could not be filled with even more material things. But you keep buying stuff anyway, as the act of buying things seems to help distract you from the fact that you feel so unfulfilled with your life.

This book on minimalism was written for people just like you, who have grown tired of a lifestyle that is centered on buying more, owning more, and working more in order to earn more and buy even more stuff. You will learn the advantages of having fewer possessions to care for and derive joy from, the ways in which your belongings prevent you from following your life pursuits, the minimalist habits to apply to different areas of your home and life, the pleasure you will get from getting rid of clutter and giving them up for others' enjoyment, and the happiness you will experience after ending up with a home that lets you live your version of the good life.

Thanks again for downloading this book, I hope you enjoy it!

1

Defining Minimalism: What It All Boils Down To

Minimalism can easily be defined as living a life that is purposefully pared down to the most basic necessities. But that short answer does not give justice to what minimalism truly is all about. It helps to think of minimalism in terms of the following ideas:

Resist and Reject

Minimalism is intentionally resisting the temptation to acquire more possessions so that you have more space — and time — in your life to allot to more significant endeavors. To be a minimalist is to actively reject the notion that having more is key to a better life. Living minimally is realizing that the essentials are all you really need in your life.

Enough is Enough

You can also think of minimalism as being freed from the overwhelming passion to possess as much as you could. It is knowing and understanding that one cannot find happiness in the latest smartphone or bottles of your favorite perfume. Minimalism helps you determine what you simply want and what you really need, as well as find the point where you have enough of what you need. Minimalism enables you to figure out that enough is enough, find the will to get off the consumerism track, and seek true happiness in your relationships and experiences.

Done With Modern Mayhem

Practicing minimalism allows you to break free from the grasp of modern life. Minimalism helps you escape the long, hurried, and stressful hours you have to put into your work so that you can pay your bills and buy even more stuff, while falling deeper into a debt trap. Minimalism lets you perform your tasks in a way that you actually enjoy doing them as well as helps you get all of those tasks done without feeling like you have lost touch with yourself, your family, and with life in general. Ultimately, minimalism helps you disengage from a fast-paced but not necessarily productive lifestyle so that you could pay more attention to the things that truly matter.

Sweet Spot

Embracing the minimalist lifestyle allows you to live the life you want — whenever and wherever you want to. Without actually intending to, most individuals end up living in duplicity. You may live a certain way when you are with your family, another way when you are in the office, and yet another way when you are around your neighbors. You may find yourself portraying a life that depends on the setting or situation you find yourself to be in. It is easy to feel stressed and disheartened that you need to "put on" different personas to meet what is expected of you by your spouse and kids, co-workers and boss, and friends and neighbors. Thankfully, minimalism lets you do away with the duplicitous life. A minimalist lifestyle lets you live just one way, wherever and with whoever you might be.

Clean Slate

Living like a minimalist is about clearing out all the excesses in your life, which means you end up having only the things that are essential and that make you feel most contented. Minimalism helps you get rid of the distractions that hinder you from working on the best project possible, eliminate the outside (and forced-upon) obligations that keep you from spending quality time with your family, and clearing away the noise that clouds your thinking, spirituality, and inner peace. The clean slate that minimalism offers is the place where you find — as well as create more joy and peace within — yourself.

Outside-In Lifestyle Change

The minimalist lifestyle is less about simply cleaning out junk from your house and more about benefitting from living with less stuff. Once you have pared down your possessions to the essentials, you will quickly realize that the external advantages, such as finding exactly what you need in the shortest possible time, will naturally lead you, making your minimalist journey a more personal and meaningful one. Instead of just getting rid of extra, unnecessary "things," you begin to search for ways you could also get rid of extra, unnecessary debts and obligations. Far from being a lifestyle that lets you decide what you should have and should not have, minimalism becomes a part of who you are.

Financial Savvy

Choosing to live a minimalist life lets you achieve financial stability, especially when you are committed to the idea of buying and accumulating only those things that are useful and meaningful to you. It does not mean that you will no longer spend money, but it does mean that you are now focused on enjoying to the fullest the few things you have decided to put your money on.

Prioritized spending: Embracing the minimalist lifestyle makes you realize which possessions hold the most importance in your life, and this realization inevitably carries over to the ways you use your money in purchasing things.

Because minimalism encourages you to focus more on experiences instead of the accumulation of particular items, it is only natural that your spending habits change for the better.

Experiences over material stuff: Minimalism helps you limit the number of items you own, which leads you to spending less on acquiring those items. This helps you build up more money that can go towards your other financial goals, such as going on your dream vacation in another country or being able to retire early with a considerably hefty nest egg.

Reduced mortgage/rent expense: The minimalist lifestyle enables you to need less space to house your carefully curated possessions. Because you will be buying a smaller house or renting a smaller apartment or studio, you can save enough money that can go towards ensuring that you have a well-designed, cozy space to live in.

Established budget for emergencies: You could be the type of person who maintains a modest emergency fund and who sees to it that you are not stuck worrying about how to pay the bill in case your hot water system blows or your car suddenly tanks. You may be someone who is always prepared to handle every small disaster that might come your way. But when you embrace the minimalist life, you will realize that your perception of financial stability takes on a different, much improved level.

• You will learn the importance of doing away with short-lived happiness at the moment for the sake of ensuring that your future finances are well taken care of. This could mean putting away 3 to 6 months' worth of funds to see you through when things get tough, such as if you suddenly lose your job. You will realize that although building an emergency fund is no walk in the park, the knowledge that you are secure in your finances does make living a minimalist lifestyle worth your while.

• Minimalism encourages you to be well-prepared for any unexpected developments in your life since you have several months' worth of funds safely stashed away, which you will use to tide you over while you are in the process of, say, looking for a new job. You become more focused on getting yourself out of a tight situation because you are not fretting over where your next meal will be coming from.

Time and money value: The minimalist lifestyle teaches you to put more value to your time and money, which spurs you to look for more efficient ways to spend the money you worked hard for. This could mean deciding to reduce your expenses, which leads you to reduce the time you spend earning the money that would have gone to paying off those done-away-with expenditures — although this does not necessarily translate to cutting back on your spending.

· Minimalism also teaches you to spend a portion of your valuable time on looking for discounts on your phone bills, as well as on your utility, insurance, and registration bills. All those money you save up from availing of these discounts go a long way toward growing your budget, and all it really took you was asking for an online quote or making a quick call. You can also save time and money at the same time by opting to have your savings transfers automated, which ensures that your saved money goes to a separate account faster than you could start imagining the ways you could spend it.

· Minimalism allows you to invest small chunks of your valuable time in searching for ways you could cut back on your expenditures, so that you can reduce the time needed to work your way toward earning that money as well as improve the way you handle your finances to ensure you are continually building up your financial stability.

Debt reduction: Minimalism curbs your appetite for debts. Embracing the minimalist life helps you realize the insidious hold that debt has on people. Some would not think twice about taking another humongous loan to purchase another vehicle right after they have paid out the first car loan. People have become so used to constantly repaying debts that they fail to consider the more important things they could have used their money on if they only held on to their slightly older but still useful and functioning means of transportation.

• Minimalism changes your mindset about taking on debts and actually makes you want to steer clear of going into debt. You become empowered to decrease and eventually pay off your current debts at the soonest possible time. Now that your credit card, for example, has been reduced, you end up having more cash to add to your savings and your overall financial security. Minimalism has you thinking that if you do not have the cash to purchase something, then you should not even think about buying it. Moreover, that emergency fund you have set aside from your spend-less-on-things lifestyle helps you avoid having to use a credit card if you ever find yourself in a tight financial situation.

• Minimalism helps you avoid living above your means. Living above your means refers to funding your lifestyle beyond what your income allows you to so that you end up sinking deep into debts. Minimalism lets you see that you can manage to find joy in having less while securing your financial future, no matter the size of your income.

Doable

Absolutely doable — that is what minimalism is. What it involves is merely eliminating the stuff you have no need of so you end up living a simple and clutter-free life in equally simple and clutter-free surroundings. To live a minimalist life means doing away with the drive of accumulating material things as well as taking on too much and trying to do everything.

Minimalism only requires you to use simple tools and wear simple clothes in performing only those tasks that absolutely need to be done.

WHAT MINIMALISM IS NOT ABOUT

Now that what minimalism means — in many different ways — has been covered, it is worth considering what minimalism is not. So many misconceptions abound about what minimalism is, such as the following:

All or Nothing

To practice minimalism has nothing to do with doing away with all the material things you have in your possession. While it is correct to say that getting rid of stuff plays a big role in living a minimalist life, minimalism is less about what you are eliminating from your life and more on the gains you reap for getting rid of stuff that do not add value to your quality of living. Minimalism has you pay more attention to the beneficial results of letting go of certain things instead of mulling over those things you are doing away with. Suffice to say that minimalism encourages you to let go in order to gain more space, more freedom, more time, and more peace. This is the reason it is wrong to think that practicing minimalism forces you to deprive yourself of certain things. You are simply giving up something to make way for the more important things.

A Hard Life

Another misconception about minimalism is that you will be living a hard life due to minimalism's restrictive nature. Some people think that minimalists live an inconvenient life as they make do with the barest of essentials after stripping their houses of all stuff that help make life easier.

The truth is that living minimally actually makes living such an easy, uncomplicated thing to do. When you practice minimalism, you reduce the time spent on cleaning up after things, not to mention the time spent on picking them up, organizing them, and looking after them. Minimalism frees up your time and space from all those things you previously thought to have been making

7

your life easier and more convenient.

Minimalism is hardly about living a hard life. Instead, it is about letting go of possessions that you do not use often, do not help in making your life convenient, and are simply creating clutter in the home.

Penny Pinching

Being a minimalist does not equate to being a frugal person. While the latter refers to carefully spending your money and looking for ways to save more of it, the former involves spending less as you purchase more purposefully, which leads you to being a more careful spender and saving more money in the process.

You could say there is a point where frugality overlaps with minimalism, especially when they both encourage you to be purposeful about the way you use your money. There are actually individuals who are drawn to minimalism because they think it will help them become more frugal. The thing is, frugality and minimalism are two entirely different things. For a person practicing frugality, the aim is to accumulate more money and that is why he/she spends less. But for a minimalist, the goal is to live on less, which is why he/she spends less and ends up saving more money.

Moreover, frugal people tend to be so focused on spending less money that they would willingly make do with purchased items of less quality. Minimalists, on the other hand, put a premium on buying items of higher quality, a concept that goes well with their intention of buying less.

Lifeless Living

Others think that a minimalist could no longer enjoy taking up hobbies or having collections. But it is wrong to think that minimalism prevents a person from keeping and doing the things he/she loves and bring him/her happiness.

Minimalism is being intentional in terms of the things you want to keep. You get rid of clutter and decide to let only those things that are useful to you and that bring you joy remain in your possession.

It helps to note that moderation is key to practicing minimalism. Instead of maintaining your 10 collections, you edit everything down to just one or two of your most loved collections. A minimalist chooses to keep only his/her best pieces around — this makes it easier for him/her to highlight their importance and the happiness they bring into his/her life, as he/she had already gotten rid of the other collections that only served as clutter.

A minimalist may enjoy a certain hobby that requires him/her to use physical supplies. He/she can always maintain a small space to contain his/her hobby supplies, with the intention of filling it only with materials that he/she absolutely will use, instead of piling it up with unused, excess supplies.

As you can see, minimalism does not make you feel deprived of the things you enjoy doing or having. You are merely getting rid of all things unnecessary in order to focus on the things that spark joy in you.

Cold and Dreary

You might think that because minimalism is about keeping only the things that are essential, useful, and bring you joy, you will end up living in a cold, all-white, uninviting abode. Here's the thing: All-white décor may be the norm with a minimalist aesthetic, but it does not mean that you cannot have your own version of a minimalist design in your home. You can still fill your own minimalist rooms with a curated collection of vibrant pillows, candles, and books — those things that you hold dear, because they speak to your personality and/or they have special meanings to you.

When you practice minimalism in designing your home, you are essentially acting like your own curator. You figure out the best pieces to display in your rooms, keeping their numbers low to avoid a cluttered look as well as to highlight the beauty of your chosen pieces. You decide to keep only the things that really speak to you, not because they are what you see promoted by the latest minimalist design concept.

Now or Never

It is not true that in order to be called a minimalist, you have to abide by certain standards or rules unique to this concept or lifestyle. There may be minimalists who have chosen to follow a specific set of rules, such as wearing only 29 articles of clothing the whole year or owning only 99 items in their lifetime, but you do not have to follow those rules they have set for themselves. You have the freedom to set your own unique set of minimalist standards, and you can certainly modify those standards as you see fit, depending on the changes you experience in your life.

This is what makes minimalism such an interesting and exciting journey. While you limit yourself to owning and living with fewer things (high quality, most loved, extremely useful), you do have a say in how minimalism means and looks like to you, and it is up to you to change things up in order to accommodate your different needs at different stages in your life.

Singled Out

Minimalism is not limited to single individuals. It works for anyone who desires to practice it, including those who have families and kids. The fact is, large families are the ones who may actually reap the most from minimalism. How minimalism might appear in an unmarried person's lifestyle will be completely different from how minimalism looks like in how a family with five kids, but the goal is the same — living simply and purposefully on few, carefully chosen things and finding the most use and joy in them.

Stuff Galore

Minimalism does not apply only to material things. You can apply it to other areas in your life as well. Aside from ridding your house of clutter, minimalism applies to how you manage your finances, time, and food choices, among others.

2

How To Use Minimalism To Improve All Areas of Your Life

Minimalism can actually be downright exhilarating. You are freed from having the passion to pursue more and instead find joy in owning less. Below are the many ways you can take advantage of minimalism's benefits to give the different areas of your life a makeover.

Achieve Financial Freedom

Practicing minimalism encourages you to spend less because you commit to the idea of buying and accumulating only those things that are essential. This results in your achieving financial freedom. Spending less on buying stuff also means you spend less on caring for, fixing, and disposing of them. Eventually, your desire for owning more material things diminishes, giving you more opportunities of using your money in other financial-savvy ways.

Enjoy Domestic Calmness and Appeal

When you live in a minimalist home, you will have the pleasure of living with less clutter and less stress. This is because reduced clutter translates to reduced visual stress, distractions, and anxieties. You will certainly feel the calming vibe of your home now that it is cleared of unnecessary possessions. You will also enjoy its clutter-free look that has high visual appeal, especially when the stuff you have on display are only those that you value most and are truly proud of. Having a carefully edited home also gives you more time for rest, as you only have fewer pieces to clean and maintain.

Find Cleanup a Breeze

Speaking of cleaning your stuff, minimalism allows you to cut back on your cleanup and dedicate more time to being more productive in other areas of your life. When you have a clutter-free house, you will also find it easier to locate missing items, so you significantly reduce the time wasted in searching for them.

Consider the following benefits of having a minimalist lifestyle and home:

· Mopping and vacuuming are much quicker because you have less stuff lying on the floor.

· You will have plenty of room for preparing meals on your kitchen countertops and you will find it easier wiping those benches down, now that you have limited stuff placed on them.

· The fact that you have fewer décor pieces lets you cut back on the time dusting them.

· Now that you have fewer things inside your car, you can easily tidy up if a neighbor or friend carpools with you.

· Owning a smaller number of clothes means you will also have fewer worn and dirty garments to launder.

Enjoy More Freedom

The minimalist lifestyle allows you to feel lighter and freer. Once you learn to wean yourself away from your material possessions and focus instead on creating and enjoying more experiences with the people you love, you will noticeably feel refreshed.

Bring Less Damage to the Environment

When you commit to consuming fewer things in the name of minimalism, you empower yourself to cause less damage to the environment. Minimalist living essentially means doing away with things that are not needed or useful and ending up with a simpler and decluttered environment that is conducive to a simpler and decluttered life. For example, looking good in what you wear may be wonderful, but not if it means damaging your surroundings and robbing people and animals of the opportunity to enjoy it.

As a minimalist, you find it more sensible to own a manageable number of quality garments that can be worn for years to come than to go through too many fast-fashion articles of clothing that will fall to pieces after two to three washes.

Opportunity to Help Others

As a minimalist, you get to help less fortunate people by donating your stuff, such as toys, craft supplies, mobile phones, and old winter coats, for good causes to charitable and nonprofit organizations. You are able to experience feeling good in the knowledge that your non-essential belongings are no longer taking up room in your home and are instead being put to good use by the homeless, the elderly, veterans, and other people in need. You are also setting a good example for your children to emulate, not to mention teaching them about generosity and other valuable lessons about life that they would never have learned from watching TV or browsing the Internet. Your kids will grow up watching you make donations and changing the lives of many people.

Enjoy Quality and Promote Sustainability

Minimalism helps you think big when making decisions. You learn to pause and reflect before making any kind of purchase. This means that all of your purchases are the result of intentional and carefully thought out decisions. You become more adept at writing down your list of necessities, knowing exactly where you will be buying them, and knowing where you will be storing them once you get home. This in turn allows you to reduce the likelihood of buying things on impulse. Quality over quantity becomes the order of the day, and you practice sustainable consumption in the process.

Reduce the Burden on Others

Minimalism not only makes your life less stressful, but also makes other people's lives less burdensome as well. Think about the fact that there will be a time, such as in the case of death, when other people will have to go through every single material possession you own. You can reduce the burden on others by living minimally and simply.

Experience More Happiness

Although it may sound surprising, you will actually be happier when you own fewer possessions. You may feel your happiness increase when you purchase material stuff, but the happiness they bring is only temporary and can disappear once you get over their newness and you become used to the idea of having these items in your possession. The same cannot be said for experiences, which provide a deep-seated joy that cannot be matched by any kind of material purchase, especially when those experiences are shared with the people you love. Such experiences let you create memories with family and friends, memories that you get to talk about through the years and even share with your kids and grandkids. Those memories may not be something you could physically display in your home, but you carry them with you and you can experience the joy they bring over and over for the rest of your life.

Enjoy the Opportunity to Work on Your Passion

Moreover, all that free time you gain from cutting back on the time you spend on shopping, cleaning, organizing, and maintaining are now available for dedicating to more sensible activities. For example, the time you used to spend window-shopping or impulse-buying at the mall is now dedicated to going over your budget and checking your expenses against your financial goals. This ultimately results in your being more financially in control of your life, as well as having the freedom to take on work that you love and are passionate about.

Forsake the Need to Compare Yourself with Others

Minimalism makes you realize you have no need of keeping up with other people. You learn to appreciate the things you already have and you have decided to live on less, so there really is no need for you to do anything just to gain other people's admiration. Minimalism teaches you to be happy with your financial decisions, which you made according to your personal reasons and not for the sake of impressing your friends and/or neighbors. Living the minimalist life makes you see the fact that different individuals have different financial circumstances. Nobody truly knows how you are faring in your financials, so there is no point in "looking the part" while sacrificing your financial stability. Minimalism allows you to actually desire something that you could afford to buy and own, but frees you from making the purchase out of a need to inspire the admiration of others.

Achieve True Happiness

When you adopt the minimalist lifestyle, you have less stuff in your possession that own you and you will have more time to spend on the things that mean most to you. Minimalism teaches you to let go of other people's expectations of you and your life, whether it is about having the most impressive career, living in the largest home, or driving the latest car. These expectations actually shift your focus away from the things that truly matter to you and that make you happy because you are hung up on doing everything possible in order to impress other people. By living minimally, you let go of the notion that other people's expectations determine your worth and focus your time and energy instead on prioritizing your personal needs.

Let Bygones Be Bygones

Minimalism helps you break away from the past so that you can plan for your future. Your day-to-day minimalist living encourages you to think of what the future holds for you, especially in terms of finances. You become more aware of how your current spending habits or patterns could affect how you might fare in the years ahead, and this forces you to take steps to ensure that the "future you" will be someone who lives a comfortable, contented life. Minimalism also helps you plan ahead and be prepared for any emergency that might come your way.

Set Your Heart on More Meaningful Things

Another benefit of living a minimalist life is that you can make room in your heart for more emotional investments and less on material possessions. You will start investing more of your time, life, and money on your relationships with family and friends, on raising your kids, and even on social causes. As you invest your heart on things that truly matter, you will no longer have your entire day ruined because your vehicle got scraped this morning.

Live Contentedly in Smaller Spaces

Instead of forever renovating and upsizing the home you want (add another room here, expand the kitchen this year, install more cabinets next year), you will appreciate the value of living in a small, but still big enough home that you need and will not force you to take out a sinfully huge second mortgage. After having cleared your house of clutter, then donating and selling those cleared-out items, you will see that the current big house you are living in is just way too big! Plus, deciding to live in a smaller dwelling helps you reduce your mortgage payments, which in the long run helps you save money for other needs.

Become Better at Parenting

Minimalism does not only apply to your material possessions. It also enables you to accomplish something crucial in your life — be a better parent to your kids.

• When you follow a minimalist lifestyle, you become empowered to be more serious with your parenting role. You are encouraged to focus more and to treat your everyday moments with your children with priority.

• Minimalism helps you remember to give importance to your time and schedule, as well as to decline plenty of things for the sake of your kids. As a parent, you may sometimes have this feeling that you are required to bring your kids to all of their activities and to enroll them in all kinds of sports that they may be interested in. But minimalism reminds you that no one can possibly do everything, even for their own kids. You will learn that you need to just say no to certain things — no matter how good they are — in order to be able to say yes to more pressing and more important things. Minimalism teaches you become the gatekeeper of your time and schedule.

• Minimalism forces you to be more careful with choosing which battles to fight with your kids. As a parent, you are all too familiar with those Hunger Games-esque episodes that you often have with your kids over the clothes they wear, the friends they hang out with, the music they listen to, the movies they watch, the language they use (especially around you), and the activities they spend their free time on. Minimalism teaches you which issues are worth standing your ground for, and which are simply not worth your time and effort. Adopting a minimalist approach to parenting helps you make up your mind about the things that matter most in your relationship with your children and then let those things drive your decisions.

• Admittedly, parenting your kids is a mentally exhausting job. But minimalism helps you realize that it is impossible to become the perfect parent. By owning and living with less stuff, you get to see how unrealistic your expectations of yourself are and how they greatly affect your mental health.

• Minimalism helps you learn to be better at finances and be more sensible at providing financially for your kids. It is typical for parents to desire to buy their kids all those stuff that they themselves were never able to own and enjoy growing up. But with a minimalist mindset, you will realize that if your kids are in possession of 99 toys, buying one more does not add value to their lives and does not increase their happiness.

Run a Better Business

Living a minimalist life can greatly affect — and benefit — your business. This is because when you are happy with fewer stuff, your life opens up to taking on new business goals. With reduced expenses, you are free to make your entrepreneurial passions a reality. And with your financial fears eliminated, overcoming any obstacle in pursuing your business goals becomes easy.

But there are other ways that minimalism helps you in your business:

• Minimalism allows you to be more resourceful and creative, and helps you realize that the best tools you can use to run your business are the ones that you already have. For instance, although you know you have the know-how to develop your own software (something that takes up a lot of your time), you would rather make use of existing software that you know will cater to your entrepreneurial needs. This way, you save a lot of time and money making new tools and get to spend them instead on improving your business.

• Minimalism can extend to how you manage your business. It forces you to really look at your business in all aspects: You will consider whether the requirements or processes you put in place are actually keeping the people who work for you from performing effectively at their job. You will reflect on the possibility that you may have overburdened your team to the point that your business has veered away from your mission. You will see the value of sharing responsibility with your team, which empowers them to do their job better and gives you the freedom to concentrate on accomplishing your business's bigger goals in the long run.

• Applying minimalism to your business lets you see the benefits of keeping it small and more manageable. By staying small, you are able to develop offerings to your clients that are unique and noticeably better compared to similar offerings from your business rivals.

3

How To Adopt a Minimalist Lifestyle

Minimalism is simply a way of making yourself happier with what you already have and letting go of things that you do not need. The question is: How can you adopt the minimalist lifestyle?

Below are the ways you can do just that:

Weigh in on Your Goals

Take a good look at how many goals you have in life and decide to reduce those goals to just one or two. By doing so, you will have more time to spend on each goal and help yourself become more likely to succeed. Write down the things that you feel are worth accomplishing in your life, then select the two that speak most to you. Once you are done achieving one goal, simply add another from the list of goals you have written down.

Be Critical of Your Possessions

Having a large number of material things in your possession only complicates your life — it saps you of your energy (all that cleaning and repairing), drains your bank account, and causes you to lose focus on more important things in life. Your possessions prevent you from spending quality time with the people you hold dear and hold you back from living your life according to your personal values. Minimalism enables you to eliminate everything that is not essential in your life.

Know that every single thing you own costs money, regardless of how small or how big the amount you spent on buying it. Besides, you also have to spend money on ensuring that each thing you bought has a storage space in your home, and that you have the energy as well as the attention for its upkeep. When you decide to own only the essential things, you have the advantage of saving lots of money from doing away with clutter costs (space, energy, and money).

Reflect on Your Time Commitments

Most people have plenty of time commitments filling their days from morning until night. Your own list of time commitments can include your job, household chores, hobbies, your children's activities, religious programs, and community events. The problem is that as the demands and expectations keep increasing, the time (hours per week) you could spend meeting them does not.

In the bigger scope of things, approaching your life in a one-commitment-after-another way hardly benefits you. The fact is, living a busy life means living an unreflective one. You may often catch yourself frantically trying to do everything expected of you that you lose the chance of sitting still long enough to even glance at your schedule. It helps to release yourself, when possible, from any time commitment that does not really add value to your life.

Let Go of Negative Thoughts

It is useless to even spare your negative thoughts and emotions the smallest bit of attention. You will never improve the quality of your life by giving in to feelings of hate, jealousy, bitterness, and resentment. What you need is to let go of these useless thoughts and focus on being happy, worry-free, stress-free, and clutter-free. Instead of filling your mind and heart with negative thoughts and emotions, fill them with positive thoughts, love, joy, and peace.

As you bask in the simplicity and clutter-free aesthetic of your minimalist home, make space only for serenity, happiness, and optimism. This process can take time and you will need to adjust to this new mindset, but it will definitely improve your life.

Get Smart with Your Debts

Make sure to take steps to reduce your debt if you are held captive by it. Quit telling yourself that your kids do not eat anything for breakfast but box cereals or that you there is no way you will skip your weekly mani-pedi even just once. Remember that in order to be freed from your debts and change your life, you will have to do away with the extras in your life and be grateful and content with the fact that you have a house to live in, clothes to protect you from the elements, a functioning car to bring you to work, and a job to sustain your essential needs (like food).

Be Mindful of Your Words

Speak less if fewer words are all you need to get your message across. Being mindful with your words means keeping your speech honest, plain, meaningful, and gossip-free. Minimalist speech also means seeing to it that you are only speaking kind words that build up other people's self-esteem and can turn fear into optimism and worries into joy; gentle words that have the power to diminish and eliminate anger; pleasant words that make people feel free, light, and open to learning (such as when dealing with your kids); and honest words that express value, trust, commitment, and love (avoid using flattery on anyone).

Watch Out for Artificial Ingredients

Stay away from refined grains like white bread, added sugar like corn syrup (high fructose), too much salt, and trans fats. When you minimize your use of these artificial ingredients, you are taking the first step to improving your energy levels and your overall health. It also helps if you cut back on your consumption, when possible, of medicines that you buy over the counter. Try your best to avoid being dependent on substances and give your body the chance to heal itself in natural ways instead.

Consider Your Screen Time

Don't allow media to rearrange your values, affect your outlook and attitude, and start dominating your life by focusing your attention away from TV, movies, video games, and other forms of technology. In order to fully appreciate your new minimalist lifestyle, you need to limit your screen time by turning off these devices.

Regard Your Connections

Although forming relationships with other people is a good thing, connecting to the world by being subjected to constant feeds of distraction is not. Know when it is time to stop reading one text message after another by turning off your phone and logging out of your social media accounts. Learn to pay attention to what is important instead of constantly focusing on what you think is urgent. You may feel important when you are bombarded with constant streams of communications from your contacts, since they make you feel that you are wanted and needed. But keep in mind that feeling important is not the same as actually accomplishing something important.

Have Second Thoughts on Multitasking

Research has shown that stress increases while productivity decreases in an individual that takes up multitasking. You might think that you have reached your peak level of efficiency by performing a number of tasks all at once. But the truth is, multitasking causes you to waste your time doing low quality work.

Besides causing you to miss a deadline and turn in sloppy work, which can get you fired from your job, multitasking has another, more worrisome consequence: stress. Trying to juggle different tasks can trigger stress and cause you to feel lousy not just about your work but also with yourself.

Eventually, simultaneously performing several tasks can endanger your health. This is why you have to rewire your brain and learn to do just one task after the other. This way, you are able to give each task the time, energy, and attention it takes to produce amazing results. Move on to the next task only once you are done with the first one.

4

Finding Your Minimalism Style

It goes without saying that your version of a minimalist lifestyle will be markedly different from others. Different people have different status (ex. single versus married), needs (with one child, many kids, no kids), place of residence (apartment, house, farm), and hobbies (stamp collection, crafts making, woodworking). Different individuals also have different collections (bottle caps, antique jewelries, stamps), forms of enjoyment (sports, movies, books, music), and cherished possessions (family heirlooms, romantic letters, old photographs).

For every individual or family, there is a minimalism style that suits their needs. The key to finding your own style of minimalism is to consider your personal values, passions, and way of thinking. It also helps to keep these tips in mind:

Know Your Reason for Living Minimally

Determine your motives for deciding to adopt the minimalist way of living. It could be because a simplified lifestyle will help you manage your health more easily, go after your dream job, have more control of your day-to-day schedule, or travel all over the globe. Write down some of the things that you desire or goals that you want to accomplish, then take note of the reason/s you believe living minimally is the way to help you achieve them. When you realize the connection between your reasons, actions, steps, and directions in embracing minimalism, everything will just fall into place.

Be in the Same Company

It helps to be surrounded by people who also embrace the minimalist lifestyle. Some people in your social circles and even in your own family may not be so keen to support you in the changes you will be making in your life. Take steps to create a minimalism-friendly environment by reading resources on minimalism such as books and blogs.

Entice, Not Force, Others to Embrace Minimalism

Instead of expecting others (or forcing them) to adopt the minimalist lifestyle as well, you can always just encourage them to try it for themselves. You may begin to do so by putting your focus on your personal possessions and being an example to others of the benefits to be gained by simplifying and being happy with less. If your desire is to have your family and friends discover the joy of owning fewer stuff, then show them the joy of having fewer stuff. To satisfy other people's curiosity about your new mindset and way of living, you could invite them to join you in a treasure hunt, minimalist-style.

Take Baby Steps

To begin your journey into minimalism, it helps to take a gradual yet steady approach. Doing so ensures that this is not going to be a brief attempt at organizing your life, but a lifestyle change.

Pick an area in your life to start applying the principles of minimalism to — not your entire life at once, which would be an unreasonable aim. That area could be a room, a closet, or a drawer — work on it and never leave it until you are finished with it.

It helps if you allow yourself to work on that area for one hour so that you avoid putting it off, especially if you do not really have a full day or weekend to work on it. Make a list of different areas to organize, then work on each item in the list every time an empty hour comes around.

Expect Discomfort

You may encounter uncomfortable situations as you slowly evolve into your chosen minimalist lifestyle — think vacant calendars and bare closets. The discomfort you feel may cause you to buy more stuff and cram more activities into your schedule. But the best thing you can do to ease your pain is to simply ponder on the ways you truly want to make use of your valuable time. Identify the things that are most important in your life. Replace shopping sprees with self-care sessions and always remember that any discomfort you are feeling will pass.

Challenge Yourself

Take pleasure in challenging yourself to spend less, own less, and live with less stuff. Buy only those things you need, keeping in mind that having the means to buy something does not translate to being obligated to buy it. Try the no-shopping challenge — do not buy anything for 30 days, do not visit the mall for two months, or do not make any clothes purchase for 120 days. Consider your needs when challenging your consumerism boundaries.

Live the Life You Want NOW

The minimalist lifestyle may be about living without clutter and stress, but this does not mean living in the simplest possible way. You are embracing the minimalist way of life in order to live the kind of life you desire, free from the extras that are unnecessary and take away your focus from the things that matter most to you. Start living now, instead of waiting for each space in your house to be clutter-free or for all of your debts to get completely paid off.

Go with Your Gut Feeling

You know what works best for you, so don't overly concern yourself about other people's advice on how to embrace the minimalist lifestyle. There are no rules about having to copy the outfits of a popular figure who extols the benefits of minimalism, owning the same car as your favorite expert on decluttering, fitting all your possessions inside a backpack, or residing in your own tiny house. Avoid worrying about the number of belongings you have or don't have. Never compare the changes you have made in your lifestyle to others.

5

APPLYING MINIMALISM TO DIFFERENT AREAS OF YOUR LIFE

The following are several areas in your life where you can apply minimalism:

Finances

When you apply minimalism to your finances, you will realize that you will gain more opportunities for putting your money to better use than merely spending it. As you become engrossed with the idea of having less and as the lure of spending fades, you will find it easy to search for ways you could use your money for more important reasons than cleaning out the sales rack at the mall. Soon, you will also discover new ways you could extend a helping hand to others.

Work

Applying minimalism at work helps you understand that you can live happily with fewer things, especially when they allow you to meet your needs and still end up with extras that you could give to others. Your view of money will shift, and so will your purpose for working. You will begin to see work as a means to add value to the lives of other people, not just as a means of paying off your monthly credit card payments.

Fitness

Many people nowadays have become obsessively preoccupied with fitness and health in ironically unhealthy ways. You might see them spend huge amounts of money — which go toward helping an industry that earns a billion dollars a year flourish — on gym memberships, fad diets, and harmful supplements. Due to aggressive and effective marketing, they have come to believe that buying into these things is a must.

But being fit and healthy should not just be about losing excess weight or building a muscular physique. Being healthy the minimalist way means focusing on your daily journey, not on a particular goal you want to achieve. Applying minimalism to your health is also about getting your body to move in ways that you enjoy, such as playing Frisbee with your family, dancing with your friends, or walking your dog, and not about forcing yourself to huff and puff with weights, running under the heat of the sun, or other things that may actually discourage you to even think about exercising. The key to achieving fitness with your minimalist lifestyle is to do things consistently; any benefit, like losing weight, is just a wonderful side effect.

Diet

Trying to eat a healthy diet can seem complicated, especially if you tend to follow fad diets every three months or so. But research has already identified the ingredients for a healthful diet (that goes well with your minimalist lifestyle): A variety of real foods, including vegetables, fruits, fish, seafood, eggs, meat, poultry, legumes, beans, dairy, seeds, and nuts — all of which should be minimally processed. It also helps to keep in mind several things:

Eat more of veggies and fruit, occasionally treat yourself to your favorite foods, and stop eating once you feel full (but not stuffed).

Relationships

When you live the minimalist lifestyle, you will find yourself having more opportunities to form new relationships with others. Becoming involved with your community and neighbors comes more easily, having visitors come to your house is no longer as nerve-wracking as before, and spending more time with friends is possible. Overall, you will start appreciating and being willing to foster your relationships.

Digital Life

Minimalism can be applied to your digital life as well, which most probably needs a major cleanup right now. Besides giving you a clean and organized set of digital tools to work with, digital minimalism helps ease your mind and streamline your workflow. Just remember that applying minimalism to your digital life is hardly a one-time event, as digital junk quickly accumulates again the moment you are done decluttering it.

Spirituality

Spirituality is another area in your life that minimalism could be applied to. Freeing your mind from the lure of advertisements leads you to appreciating the benefits of solitude and meditation. Minimalism helps draw you nearer to a higher power — not necessarily resulting in a change of faith, but bringing new depth to what you believe in.

Pursuit of Happiness

Apply minimalism to your heart and you will find it opened to happiness, gratitude, contentment, and generosity. Your pursuit of happiness no longer takes place inside the malls or boutiques, as you now find happiness right inside your own home, in the company of family and friends, and in the experiences and memories you create with them.

6

MINIMALIST HOME DECLUTTERING HABITS

Now that you know what minimalism is, what it does for you, and where you may apply it, you can finally start your minimalist living journey. Begin by adopting these minimalist habits:

MINIMALIST HOME DECLUTTERING HABITS

Clutter everywhere and clutter that just keeps on mounting — you might say clutter is the stuff that most homes are made of. But this does not have to be the case with your own home, especially when you have these mess-busting tips to guide you. Soon you will be basking in the minimalist glory of your orderly household.

Ready…

1. Establish your home decluttering goals.

You need to have a plan prior to starting to declutter your home, and the step you need to take in order to formulate that plan is to be clear with your goals. To get you started, it helps to bear the following in mind:

· Make a list or draw a map that includes every room as well as every clutter hub in your house.
 · Allot the necessary amount of time to each space in your house by giving it a grade, depending on how severe the clutter is.
 · Decide to tackle one space or room at a time.
 · Figure out realistic dates by which you should be finished with each stage of your decluttering goals. Make sure those dates are attainable, although making things a bit challenging might help decluttering feel more enjoyable than burdensome.

2. Get your sorting system all sorted out.

A sorting system helps you to more easily and more quickly segregate the items you come across while going through each space or room in your home. Try the 3-box method, wherein you immediately decide what to do with an item the moment you find it. This prevents you from having to deal with a bigger sorting mess later.

· Take 3 big boxes. Tape a "Keep" label on one box, a "Toss" label on another box, and a "Store" label on the last one.
 · Go through one room in the house and fill each of the three boxes with the appropriate items.
 · After going through one room, empty all of the three boxes right away.
 · Place the "Keep" items in their respective drawers, containers, or other

designated spots and label if necessary.

· Sort the "Toss" items into those you will be selling and those you will be giving away, then store in the attic/garage before it is finally time to get rid of them.

· Place all items in the "Store" box in a storage container, which you will label before putting away in a storage area.

3. Determine the exact ways you will dispose of your "Toss" items.

Consider the following strategies for getting rid of your toss-able clutter:

· Have them recycled. If you are lucky enough to have curbside pickup, then ensure that all recyclable paper, plastics, and glass go right into the recycling bin. If not, then place all the recyclable items in bags that you can transport later to your local recycling drop-off station/kiosk.

· Give them to others who need them. Instead of throwing away your still-useful trash, give them a new lease on life by donating them. You can donate your household items as well as articles of clothing that are still in good condition to the nearest local charity. You might also consider uploading images of said items on a website where people could see and get your "trash" and turn them into their own treasures.

· Sell them to others who want them. The easiest way to make money off your trash is to hold a garage sale. Ensure lots of foot traffic to your garage sale by participating in your homeowners' association's or neighborhood's garage sales events.

· Have them hauled away. Cut yourself some slack and have your trash hauled away through a rented dumpster. This is especially helpful if your tossed items are too many to handle on your own.

4. Have the following organizing tools on hand:

· Trash bags for collecting the items you will discard or donate. Of course, you need to see to it that all of those bags leave the house.

· Label maker to label every drawer and container to remind yourself as well as other family members what items are exactly contained in them.

· Nice boxes for storing the items you tend to frequently use. You may then stack, label, and display said boxes.

· File folders for broadening your file categories. Otherwise, your filing turns into a burdensome activity that you would most likely want to avoid doing.

5. Remember to always tackle the task you least like — this will help you feel that you have truly accomplished something, which will motivate you to do even more decluttering around the house.

Set...

Decluttering can become an overwhelming task if you let your emotions get the better of you. If you are having a hard time parting ways with your beloved junk, heed these mental preparation tips:

1. Decide to toss away items — be they clothes, books, or gadgets — that you only use 20% of the time.

2. Never mind the cost of each item you toss, which you can never be able to recover. What you should do is figure out if keeping it around will add value to your life or not.

3. If something is no longer functional, toss it out. If it is something you want to try repairing, by all means do so, but only if you decide to use it instead of letting it sit and gather dust.

4. Remember the last time an item was used. If six months have passed without you ever having even seen that item, then it must be time you are

finally getting rid of it.

5. Keep track of the items you do use. If something has not been used for a year, toss it.

6. Place items in the "Toss" box or bin if you do not love them enough to actually use them in the last six months.

7. After putting things into your "Get Rid" container, spend one night sleeping on your decision to eliminate them from your life. If something is calling for you to "save" it the next morning, take it out of the "Get Rid" container and place it in its newly designated storage spot.

8. Encourage yourself to really dig into your decluttering endeavors by tackling two to three small projects at first.

9. Make your decluttering objectives much easier to accomplish by simply clearing off all flat surfaces such as shelves and countertops and then keeping all like things close to one another.

10. Strive to keep away any future clutter.

• Ask yourself if you absolutely need something before you decide to buy and bring it into your home.
   • Perform mini-cluttering tasks daily, especially with your clothes, toys, mail, and other common household items that are notorious for creating the most clutter. If going over these items everyday is not manageable, try doing it every weekend instead.
   • Follow the rule of "In One Comes, Out One Goes." Each time you bring an item inside your home, make sure to get rid of another item by donating or throwing it out.
   • Practice borrowing or renting something instead of buying it if you are going to use it on rare occasions. As for video games, books, and other clutter-

prone thingamajigs, consider enjoying their digital versions.

11. Once you have decluttered one area in your home, make a pledge to never store anything in it ever again.

12. Live with certain flaws in your decluttering projects, especially in the beginning. Your house may end up far from being perfectly minimalist, but you will definitely sense a feeling of order and ease after decluttering.

Go!

1. Bring any junk mail to the recycling bin right away. It helps to check the mail's natural flow in your house. Make sure most of your junk mail do not even have the chance to reach the counter by having a recycling bin situated before the area where your mail gets dropped off. Doing so also makes you less likely to think about the advertisements contained in all that junk mail — a welcome bonus!

2. Your closet may have turned into a treasure trove of one-use articles (such as your shimmering wedding dress or show-stopping prom night number) as well as unique vintage finds — which could only mean that your closet is absolute chaos. Organize it now by having all these items professionally cleaned before storing in boxes or on hangers. If you plan on storing these clothes in boxes, choose the acid-free cardboard ones (do not forget to use acid-free paper in wrapping each crease or fold). If you would rather hang them, make sure you are going to do so using quality hangers (remember to use muslin in wrapping each garment). Segregate these items from your regular items and make sure to go over them on a yearly basis to check for any damage.

3. Ensure your kitchen appliances are safely stored out of sight. These

appliances include your coffee maker, toaster, and can opener — all of which take up considerable space. It may seem like they do not really take up that much area in the kitchen, but try working on the counter while you prepare dinner and you will surely see how less constricted your movements become. To think that all it takes for you to put these gadgets away each morning, so long as each of them already has a designated storage spot, is a mere five seconds or so.

4. Take out 10 clothing items from the closet and place them immediately inside a box. These clothes should be those you have not worn for a really long time. After five minutes of doing this step, you will have yourself a closet in which all the remaining clothing items fit better and are able to breathe. As for that box, label it and then drop off at the nearest Goodwill. Repeat this process as needed.

5. Immediately take action on your clean clothes and dirty clothes. These items are notorious for creating one of the biggest clutters in a household. Get rid of the habit of throwing your dirty clothes on the floor after taking them off; instead, drop them right away into the clothes chute or laundry basket. Meanwhile, hang each clean article of clothing back on its respective hanger or fold and arrange in its designated drawer.

6. Declutter your kitchen by storing every item near the spot you will be using it. This could mean you will place your dinnerware on the side table near the dining table, the pans and pots right beside the stove, and the dinnerware alongside the dishwasher. Doing so helps create a more relaxing atmosphere in your kitchen as well as make it easier for you to figure out which items are not utilized every day, which items are not actually needed, and which items will have to be stored in another part of the house. As for the stuff that you do frequently use, make sure to store them nearest where your work counters are (this could mean the cabinets just above the counters or the drawers right below).

7. Note that your kids' toys belong to the confines of a closet and not on a floor or dresser. In case the toy closet gets too full, then it is time to donate some of the unused ones to make room for the remaining toys. It is definitely easier to take out the toys from the closet if the latter is not crammed beyond its capacity.

8. Teach your kids to put away their playthings every evening. Making this your kids' nightly assignment provided the following advantages:

· Your kids learn how to be responsible for their belongings.
  · Your kids see the beauty of not having so many toys.
  · Your home gets cleaned before you all turn in for the night.

9. Have a field day filling your garbage cans and recycling containers. Take out the dusty junk sitting in your attic, get all old toys out of the kids' rooms, remove stale food from your pantry, and take out the no-longer-useful paperwork you brought home from the office — then place everything in your trash containers. You can do this on a weekly basis, or you can make this an every-other-week habit — it is all up to you.

10. Your toilet bath furniture will be a good spot to park your towels, toiletries, and extra toilet paper. If keeping the toilet seat in the down position is not possible, go for a unit that comes with closed shelving or cabinets.

11. Creating a more streamlined look for your kitchen — as well as ensuring that its design is conducive to more efficient activity — helps to put as much focus on what is inside your drawers and cabinets as you do on their elegant exterior colors or attractive veneer. If gutting your kitchen is not on your list of priorities, you can still manage to improve it by simply having the storage interiors upgraded. In doing so, it is important that you take into account the items that will go inside and the manner in which you will access them. After, you can decide whether you need to upgrade to drawer dividers, vertical tray dividers, or roll-out shelves.

12. Save yourself a trip to the store and make use of old shoe boxes, gift boxes, cereal boxes, and plastic bins you already have in the house. Use these to hold your found items while decluttering through each room or space.

13. Follow the 3-step method of sorting papers.

· Toss the "Trash" piles of paper in the trash bin.
  · Keep the documents you need on "File."
  · Place the To-Do piles in a separate filing system.

14. Sort your DVD or book collection, then donate or sell those pieces that no longer fit your style or theme.

15. Throw out old remote controls that no longer function, or take them to the nearest recycling center.

16. Tame your cords using these life-saving tips:

· Use washi tape in labeling your cords — they make telling which cord goes with which device much easier.
  · Use binder clips to hold frequently unplugged cords together on top of your desk.
  · Tie together your excess cables using rubber bands or twist ties.
  · Make sure to use cables and cords that are just the right lengths.
  · Opt for furniture pieces that are designed to hide cords, especially if you do not like the idea of feeding cords into the wall.
  · Place your cords in a colored storage container that matches the color theme of your room.
  · Use an area rug to cover up some cords.

17. Declutter the bedroom closet in three easy steps:

· One: Remove every piece of clothing.

· Two: Sort everything.

· Three: Return what you will still be wearing and throw out or donate those that you no longer will.

18. Follow these tips on decluttering the countertop in your bathroom:

· Put together your toiletries on an attractive tray. What's great about using a tray to hold such items is that you get to create boundaries that help prevent your jars and bottles from taking over the whole countertop. Although it would be nice to have trays that are specially designed for bath storage use, you will find that any type of tray that can fit on the counter will be spacious enough to hold your toiletries. Just make sure to use a tray that is moisture-safe, can be easily cleaned, and comes in a design or color that matches your bathroom motif.

· Utilize drawer trays to hold your bobby pins, headbands, toe spacers, and other dust-gathering miscellaneous items that you usually toss on your bathroom countertop. Keep them nicely sorted by arranging them in separate drawer trays — the ones typically used in organizing home office supplies and kitchen paraphernalia. You might also consider using translucent plastic bins for the same purpose, making sure to tuck them inside a cabinet.

· Install a shelf in your bathroom. All you need is one slim wall shelf to greatly improve your bathroom. You can add a basket to serve as a catchall bin if you would rather not have your bathroom knickknacks on full display. In case you have considerable wall space (like near the bathtub), you can install on it a bookshelf that can serve as a storage unit for your bathroom supplies as well as a piece of décor or two.

· Keep your loose items like cotton swabs and cotton balls stored in handy canisters. This ensures that these necessities stay organized while being kept sanitary. You can have fun choosing from a wide array of tea tins, mason jars, and apothecary jars and then putting them on display in your bathroom. If you do not like the idea of placing these canisters in clear view, you can always place them inside one of your vanity cabinets.

· Have wall-mounted holders installed inside the bathroom. You can free up plenty of space around your bathroom sink if you go for toothbrush holders and soap dispensers that you just attach to a wall. Take things a decluttering step further by purchasing a multipurpose holder that can hold toothbrushes, soaps, tumblers, and other items.

19. In case your collection of necklaces has gotten so out of hand that there is not enough room for you to even move them around in order to find a specific piece, you might be better off storing your neck candies on a hanging organizer. Choose one that you just snap or clip onto a hanger. It also helps if you use one that comes with lots of clear pockets to avoid getting anything all tangled up.

20. Get your home office decluttered and more efficient by zoning it into 3 specific areas of activity:

· The work area, where the computer, your most-often used office equipment, and a clear workspace are located

· The reference area, where professional books, manuals, dictionaries, binders, and other office materials could be found

· The supply area, where paper supplies and other office supplies are stored

21. You may noticed that, while you have a food processor, crock pot, waffle iron, egg slicer, and other small gadgets to help you work around the kitchen, you usually just grab your knife to help you do myriad jobs. Your kitchen appliances just end up taking up space on your counters and accumulating dust, making them even harder to clean. Decide which of these items of convenience should remain in your kitchen. As for the rest, safely store them out of the way.

22. Instead of displaying all your mementos all at once, try putting on view just a few items, which makes for a more striking and interesting effect. Consider your photos not just as great reminders of a special event in your life, but also as your living room décor.

23. Take advantage of wastebaskets in order to cut back on the amount of clutter your household accumulates, especially in your family room. If you are afraid of putting a wastebasket in the family room because it tends to smell bad and look unattractive, consider going for a trashcan that complements the décor in the room. If you know your kids will be eating there, make sure to purchase a trashcan that comes with a tight lid, and make sure to line it with deodorizing trash bags.

24. You may have trouble locating your bathroom counter space with all the mane stuff that litter its surface — think combs, sprays, hair dryers, curlers, and brushes. Organize them as quickly as you can by simply loading all your bathroom supplies into a plastic tub, which you can fit under the sink. But be mindful of what you do put inside the tub: In goes anything that you often use, and everything else can go to charity or a friend who would be delighted to use them. Then, when it is time to do your 'do, simply take the entire tub out; later, just put it back under the sink.

25. Commit to designating a spot for every item inside your closet. Make sure all your footwear are placed together in one area, your jeans in another area, and so forth. This way, you maintain your closet's decluttered look while you are saved from the hassle of figuring out what to wear every morning. Figure out how to make use of every inch inside the closet — you could have twice as much storage if you install shelves (this actually helps your T-shirts, sweaters, and other knitwear retain their shape).

26. Your towel rack is probably not big enough to accommodate all the towels that your family members go through. You can install hooks inside the bathroom to address this problem. You will find these hooks cheap, space-savvy, and easy to mount. Finally, the bathroom floor won't get damp anymore from all those towels that keep falling, and there will be no more squabbles over whose towel is whose.

27. The easiest way to store your traditional photos is to place them inside

photo boxes. You could store them by occasion or by year. Make sure to have your photos stored somewhere safe and dry so that they do not get damaged by extreme temperature changes, humidity, and moisture. Meanwhile, you can take advantage of photo websites to store your digital photos. All you have to do is open an account, keep it active, and make a purchase in order to avail yourself of unlimited photo storage.

28. Consider attaching or hanging a shoe organizer at the back of your door. This lets you have a place to easily access the stuff you usually need when going out of the house, without having them get in your way as you dash off in the morning. The shoe organizer's sizeable pockets do a good job holding scarves, pet leashes, mittens, garden gloves, shoes, and sunglasses.

29. Purchase storage bins that you could easily roll or slide under your bed. They help you maximize your bedroom's horizontal space, since they can serve as your closet's extensions. Rolling or sliding storage bins lets you rotate your seasonal garments as well as store your blankets, purses, backpacks, and other bulkier, bigger items. You can even ensure these bins stay hidden by using a bedskirt. Make things easier for yourself and other family members when figuring out what are inside these bins by labeling them on the outside.

30. If you are lucky enough to have plenty of bathroom counter space, and it would not be a bother to you to have stuff sitting there in plain sight, then try purchasing apothecary jars to hold all your stuff. You will find that your bath salts, soaps, and cotton swabs simply look elegant and clutter-free when placed in these clear glass holders.

31. Clear your dining table so you will actually have room for eating on it by:

• Stashing away your dining accessories. Keep the dining table clutter-free between meals by gathering in a sideboard your napkin holders, placemats, salt and pepper shakers, and other similar items.

  • Transfer the mail near the door. Establish an area near your door in which to process all mails to keep your dining table from nursing junk mail, greeting cards, and piles of bills. Make use of a sideboard by placing a mail-holding basket on it, as well as small boxes for files, stamps, and envelopes.

· Arrange your magazines the right way instead of letting them take over your entire dining table. Do a quick go-through of all your reading materials and identify those that you want to clip recipes or other information from, those that you want to read again, and those you want to get rid of. Arrange those magazines you want to keep by category and place them in magazine holders, which you will then set up on a storage ottoman or a bookshelf.

· Designate a station to hold your pet supplies. Your dining table can easily become a landing spot for your dog's leash after walks; avoid this from happening again by placing leashes, treats, and other pet items in stacking bins parked near the entryway.

· Give your electronic devices a new place to call home. Avoid the inconvenience of scooping out tablets, cell phones, chargers, and cords each time you need to set the dining table by establishing a designated charging station. Doing so ensures your devices are safely charged and thankfully out of your way.

· Your dining table may have become your kids' unofficial area for doing their homework. Every time they have finished working on their craft projects and other assignments, make sure to clear away the supplies right away, then put away in storage bins or baskets. It would be great if you use storage containers that easily slide out of a sideboard.

· Make over your entryway so that your kids will learn to hang their backpacks and jackets there, instead of dropping their stuff on the dining table. Have hooks installed near your front door to ensure those backpacks and jackets never make it to the dining room.

· Instead of dropping your keys on the table, where they tend to get lost, make room for a key holder (a dainty dish or a row of hooks) by the door, then make sure to place your keys there each time you enter the house.

· Stop using your dining table as a fresh laundry folding station. Overhaul your designated laundry area by placing a tall cart or a table that you could fold down in there.

• Never place your special-occasions-only china and fancy holiday décor inside the shelves, buffet, or sideboard in the dining room. Place all these items in designated storage areas and use the dining room spaces for storing only frequently used supplies.

32. Give your garage a much-needed makeover by following these decluttering strategies:

• Get all garage items out. This is the easiest way for you to assess those items as well as the amount of space you have in your garage.
  • Begin sorting through the items you cleared out of the garage, making sure to put together like items. Put together all your gardening tools in one spot, your collection of sports equipment in another spot, your camp gear in yet another spot, and your hardware tools in one area.
  • Purge your sorted garage items of any duplicates, especially those that you know you will not be using within the next 5 years. As for anything damaged or worn out, get rid of them as well. If you have any tools that were used just once, you might as well make money off them (by selling them) or make someone else happy (by giving them away).
  • Get things organized. Once you are done sorting through every item in the garage and figuring out which items are for keeps, decide how you are going to store them in the most space-maximizing ways possible. This could mean you will need to buy additional storage bins as well as a pegboard, sturdy shelving, or a tool cabinet. If possible, consider installing a garage storage rack in an upright and off-the-ground position to create more space. It also helps to put clear labels on everything you store in the garage to facilitate any searching for items down the road.

7

MINIMALIST EATING AND COOKING HABITS

Simplify the way you keep your mind and body healthy with the help of the following minimalist lifestyle-friendly eating and cooking tips:

1. Have less to eat.

Eating less is a great idea if you have issues with excess weight, but it may not be such a good idea if you are underweight. However, eating fewer calories than the majority of people has been shown to help Okinawans achieve longevity as well as incredible health. These people are known to stop eating once they are 80 percent full. You can follow suit by reducing your food portions gradually, which allows your stomach to also gradually get smaller. The trick is to take things slowly — never starve yourself.

2. Be mindful of how you eat.

Chew each bite thoroughly and concentrate on how each morsel makes you feel. Savor the taste of your meal instead of focusing on what's on TV.

3. Consume single-ingredient foods.

Whole foods are truly satisfying and nutritious, making you forget about taking a bite of processed junk foods. Have your fill of high quality, healthy foods with names that you could easily pronounce and that do not come with an ingredients list (the food themselves are ingredients). Eat the following with pleasure: vegetables, fruits, fish, poultry, whole grains, eggs, legumes, and nuts.

4. Make use of the simplest flavorings.

Using single ingredients of the highest quality in preparing your meals means you no longer have to add too much flavoring. You will find your meals enjoyable with just a touch of pepper, fresh herbs, salt, and olive oil. It also helps if you forego buying new flavorings if you think you will not be using that much anyway. For new recipes that will have you using condiments and spices that are difficult to find, you could just substitute it with what you currently have sitting in your pantry. Just avoid buying rare ingredients that you will most likely just use once. You would be surprised how, with a little creativity, you can use common ingredients to enhance any meal you prepare.

5. Raid your spice cabinet.

Check your collection of spices and herbs for any duplicates and ingredients that you do not use on a regular basis. Purge your disorganized spice cabinet of anything that you have never used and give them away. Pour the duplicates into a single container to free up some space inside the cabinet.

Now that you have a decluttered spice cabinet, it will become easier for you to search for a certain herb or spice, which helps you cook much faster and without fuss. Try going over your spice cabinet two to three times a year.

6. Prepare delicious meals that require just 3 simple steps.

Here are 25 recipes that warm your heart, whet your appetite, and require minimal fuss:

Bacon and Broccoli Bowls

Ingredients: bacon slices, chopped (4 slices); garlic cloves, small, chopped finely (2 pieces); Parmesan cheese, grated (2 handfuls); broccoli, frozen, defrosted (500 grams); lemon juice, freshly squeezed (1 teaspoon); olive oil (1/4 cup)

Instructions: 1) Heat a medium-sized nonstick saucepan over medium-high heat. Pour in the olive oil, then stir in the bacon and cook until crisp and browned. 2) Drain the broccoli thoroughly before tossing in with the browned bacon bits. Stir in the garlic as well, then cover and continue cooking for 2 to 3 minutes or until the broccoli is softened and heated through. 3) Turn off the heat before stirring in the grated Parmesan cheese and lemon juice.

Fried Cabbage and Eggs

Ingredients: cabbage, sliced finely (1/4 piece); eggs, large (2 pieces); soy sauce (1 tablespoon)

Instructions: 1) Heat a large nonstick skillet on medium-high before adding a small amount of oil. Stir in the cabbage, cover, and cook for 7 to 10 minutes or until the cabbage softens and loses its crunch. 2) Turn heat down to medium-low, then stir in the soy sauce and eggs. 3) Stir and cook for another 30 seconds or until the eggs are almost firm.

Scrumptious Spinach Soup

Ingredients: onions, softened (2 pieces); stock, reduced sodium (2 cups);

walnuts, roasted (2 handfuls); spinach, frozen, defrosted (500 grams); olive oil; feta cheese, crumbled (200 grams)

Instructions: 1) Fill a medium nonstick saucepan with olive oil and heat on medium. Stir in the onion and salt, cover, and cook for 10 minutes or until the onions are softened. 2) Pour in the stock and stir in the spinach. Let the mixture simmer for two to three minutes. 3) Pour soup into individual bowls and serve topped with walnuts and feta cheese.

Cheesy Olive Steaks

Ingredients: steaks, small (2 pieces); black olives, pitted, mashed (1 handful); vegetable salad (1 serving); rosemary sprig, chopped finely (1 piece); feta cheese/goat cheese, crumbled (100 grams)

Instructions: 1) Slice the steaks into 3 equal-sized portions. Roll the meat pieces with a rolling pin until they are about a quarter-of-an-inch thick. After rubbing the steaks with oil, dust with salt. 2) Heat a large nonstick skillet on medium-high. Add the seasoned steaks and cook on each side for 1 minute or until browned and cooked through. Toss in the rosemary before turning off the heat. 3) Transfer the steaks to a platter and top with olive oil as well as the feta or goat cheese and black olives.

Parsley Carrot Bowls

Ingredients: baby carrots, large (500 grams); wine/rice vinegar (2 table-spoons); neutral flavored oil (6 tablespoons); sunflower seeds, toasted (2 handfuls); carrot tops (1/2 bunch); parsley, flat leaf (1/2 bunch); Dijon mustard (1 tablespoon); chicken breast, seasoned with pepper and salt, pan-fried, sliced into cubes or strips (300 grams).

Instructions: 1) Grate the carrots and parsley in the food processor after removing the stems and legs. 2) Mix the mustard and oil with salt and vinegar in a medium bowl. Add the grated carrots and parsley and toss until well-combined. 3) Place the mixture in individual bowls and top with the cubed or sliced chicken and sunflower seeds.

Hazelnut and Chorizo Hummus

Ingredients: chorizo, crumbled/sliced (2 pieces); hazelnuts, roasted (2 handfuls); hummus (1 cup); baby spinach leaves (1 bag)

Instructions: 1) Heat a medium skillet (nonstick) on medium. Add the chorizo and cook until all sides are browned. 2) Line 2 plates with hummus. 3) Add the cooked chorizo to the hummus, then top with the salad leaves and hazelnuts.

Broccoli and Tuna Bake

Ingredients: onion, sliced finely into half-moons (1 piece); cream (1 cup); cheese, grated (2 handfuls); broccoli heads (2 pieces); tuna, canned (180 grams)

Instructions: 1) Set the oven at 480 degrees Fahrenheit to preheat. Meanwhile, cut the onion into half-moons and arrange at the bottom of a roasting pan in a single layer. 2) Chop up the broccoli (including the stems) into bite-sized chunks and layer on top of the onions. Top with a drizzling of olive oil and bake, covered with foil, for 15 to 20 minutes or until the veggies are tenderly cooked. 3) Pour in the cream and tuna and stir to combine. Add the grated cheese on top and bake for an additional 5 minutes or until nice and golden.

Hot Tomato Soup

Ingredients: onions, diced (2 pieces); tomato puree/passata (3 cups); harissa (2 tablespoons); coconut cream (15 ounces); hazelnuts, roasted (2 handfuls)

Instructions: 1) Heat a medium saucepan on medium before adding a little oil. Stir in the diced onions and cook for 10 minutes or until softened without being browned. 2) Stir in the coconut cream and tomato puree/passata. Allow the mixture to boil, then reduce heat to a simmer. Cook for 5 minutes. 3) Turn off the heat before processing the mixture with an immersion blender. Stir in the harissa and pour into individual bowls. Serve topped with hazelnuts.

Smoking Mushroom Bowls

Ingredients: mushrooms, flat, large, sliced (500 grams); olive oil, extra virgin (3 tablespoons); paprika, smoked (2 teaspoons); walnuts (2 handfuls); sour cream (for serving); salad leaves (for serving)

Instructions: 1) Set the oven at 480 degrees Fahrenheit to preheat. Meanwhile, fill a roasting pan with oil, paprika, and the mushroom slices. Toss to combine, season with salt, and cook for 10 minutes or until nicely roasted. 2) Give the mushroom mixture a good stir before adding the walnuts. Cook for an additional 5 minutes or until the mushrooms are tenderly cooked. 3) Line 2 individual bowls with the salad leaves. Add the mushroom and walnut mixture on top. Finish by topping with sour cream.

Roast Ratatouille

Ingredients: eggplant, medium (2 pieces); coriander (1 teaspoon); cumin (1 teaspoon); hummus (300 grams); zucchini, small (3 pieces); olive oil, extra virgin (5 tablespoons); salad greens (for serving)

Instructions: 1) Set the oven at 480 degrees Fahrenheit to preheat. Meanwhile, chop the zucchini and eggplant into bite-sized cubes, place in the roasting pan, and toss with the oil, spices, and salt. 2) Load into the oven to roast for 30 minutes, making sure to stir halfway. 3) Top 2 individual plates with equal amounts of hummus. Add the salad leaves and roast ratatouille.

White Beans and Chorizo

Ingredients: onion, peeled, chopped (1 piece); beans, canned, drained (14 ounces); baby spinach (1 bag); chorizo (200 grams); ketchup (4 tablespoons)

Instructions: 1) Heat a frying pan on medium before adding a little oil. Stir in the onion and cook for 5 minutes or until softened. 2) Stir in the chorizo and cook for an additional 5 minutes or until browned and cooked through. 3) Stir in the ketchup and beans and cook until the mixture is heated through. Serve alongside the baby spinach.

Broccoli and Smoked Trout Bowls

Ingredients: broccoli heads, chopped into one-inch chunks (2 pieces); trout, smoked, hot, flaked (300 grams); chives, chopped (1/2 bunch); lemon juice, freshly squeezed (4 tablespoons); sour cream (8 tablespoons)

Instructions: 1) Fill a small pot with one-inch-deep of salted water and bring to a boil. 2) Chop the broccoli into bite-sized chunks (including the leaves and stems) and drop into the pot. Cover and simmer for about 5 minutes, then drain and let cool on a tray. 3) Fill 2 bowls with the broccoli and then sprinkle on the lemon juice and the flaked fish. Serve topped with sour cream, chives, and black pepper.

Tasty Tomato Omelet

Ingredients: Butter, grass-fed (2 tablespoons); sundried tomatoes (1 handful) or bacon, cooked (1 handful); salad leaves (for serving); eggs, pastured (3 pieces); Parmesan cheese, grated (1 handful)

Instructions: 1) Combine salt (a pinch) with the eggs. Meanwhile, heat butter in a nonstick skillet heated on medium and let it melt. 2) Pour the egg mixture into the melted butter and cook for 1 to 2 minutes. Top with the cheese and tomatoes/bacon and continue cooking for another 1 to 2 minutes or until the eggs are about set. 3) Transfer the omelet onto a plate, making sure to roll it as you go. Serve alongside the salad.

Sausage and Cauliflower Soup

Ingredients: sausages, crumbled (4 pieces); cumin seeds (1 teaspoon); parsley, flat leaf, finely chopped (1/2 bunch); cauliflower (500 grams); chicken stock, reduced sodium (2 ½ cups); olive oil, extra virgin (6 tablespoons)

Instructions: 1) Heat a nonstick skillet on medium-high before pouring in oil (2 tablespoons). Unwrap the casings off the sausage and then crumble the meat and add to the hot pan. Stir and cook until the sausage is cooked and browned through. 2) Chop the cauliflower into bite-sized pieces and add to the pan, along with the stock and cumin. Stir to combine, then cover and cook on a simmer for 15 minutes. Pour into bowls. 3) Combine the parsley and olive oil. Season to taste and add on top of each bowl.

Chicken Pesto Burgers

Ingredients: chicken mince, ground (500 grams); burger buns (3 pieces); salad leaves; pesto (3 tablespoons + 3 teaspoons); mayonnaise

Instructions: 1) In a medium bowl, mix the chicken mince with the pesto (3 tablespoons) and shape into 3 equal-sized patties. 2) Dust fine salt (1/2 teaspoon) at the bottom of the frying pan, making sure to form an even layer. Add the patties and cook on each side for 3 to 5 minutes or until cooked and browned through. 3) Smear the remaining pesto (1 teaspoon) on each burger bun's base before topping with a browned patty. Finish each burger bun by adding the salad leaves and mayonnaise.

Tahini Kale Bowls

Ingredients: kale (1 bunch); tahini (4 tablespoons); hazelnuts, roasted (2 handfuls); lemon juice, freshly squeezed (2 tablespoons + 4 tablespoons);

pesto (4 tablespoons)

Instructions: 1) Remove the stems off the kale, then tear the leaves into one-inch pieces. Add fine salt (a pinch) and lemon juice (2 tablespoons) and toss until well-combined, then let sit for an hour. 2) Mix the remaining lemon juice (4 tablespoons) with the pesto and tahini. 3) Spread the prepared dressing onto 2 plates before topping with the kale and hazelnuts.

Harissa Eggplant Soup

Ingredients: eggplant, medium (2 pieces); sour cream (8 tablespoons); olive oil, extra virgin (2 tablespoons); stock, vegetable/chicken, low-sodium (2 cups); harissa (2 tablespoons); roast almonds, chopped (1 handful)

Instructions: 1) Set the oven at its highest setting. Meanwhile, slice the unpeeled eggplant into one-inch chunks and arrange in the baking tray. Sprinkle with salt and olive oil, then roast in the oven for 20 minutes, making sure to stir halfway. 2) Pour the stock into a saucepan and heat to a simmer. Add the roasted eggplant and cook for 2 more minutes. Turn off the heat before processing the mixture with a stick blender until a bit chunky. 3) Mix the olive oil with the harissa and add on top of the eggplant soup, along with the sour cream and almonds.

Easiest Macaroni and Cheese

Ingredients: pasta (200 grams); Parmesan cheese, grated (2 handfuls); cream (4 tablespoons); salad leaves (for serving)

Instructions: 1) Fill a pot with salted water and bring to a boil. Add your pasta and follow package directions in cooking it until al dente. 2) Drain the cooked pasta and add to the pot again. Combine with the grated cheese and cream. 3) Serve macaroni and cheese alongside the salad leaves.

Feta Spinach Frittata

Ingredients: eggs (6 pieces), feta cheese, crumbled (200 grams); spinach, frozen, defrosted, squeezed dry (250 grams); chili oil (1 tablespoon)

Instructions: 1) Set the oven at 350 degrees Fahrenheit. Meanwhile, grease the sides and bottom of a springform pan (oven-safe). 2) Combine eggs with the feta cheese and spinach and then pour into the greased pan. Bake for about 15 to 20 minutes or until your frittata is evenly cooked. 3) Drizzle on top with chili oil and serve immediately.

Tasty Chicken Tenders

Ingredients: wheat germ (1 tablespoon); egg, lightly beaten (1 piece); bread crumbs, whole wheat (1 cup); chicken cutlets, sliced into one-ounce strips (6 ounces)

Instructions: 1) Set the oven at 375 degrees Fahrenheit and spray a baking pan with cooking spray after lining with parchment. 2) Combine the wheat germ and bread crumbs. Coat the chicken pieces with the beaten egg before dipping in the bread crumb mixture. 3) Arrange the chicken tenders inside the prepped pan and bake for about 6 to 8 minutes.

Salmon Packets

Ingredients: parchment paper, large square (1 piece); soy sauce, low sodium (1 teaspoon); salmon fillet (1 piece); mustard (2 teaspoons); lemon slices, freshly cut (2 pieces)

Instructions: 1) Set the oven at 375 degrees Fahrenheit to preheat. 2) Place the fish on the left side of the parchment. Smear the mustard on top before drizzling with the soy sauce. Top with the lemon slices. 3) Fold the parchment's right side over the fish and seal tightly. Bake for 12 minutes.

Watercress and Ginger Mushrooms

Ingredients: ginger, fresh, grated, 1-inch (1 piece); shiitake mushrooms, w/ stems removed, cut into matchsticks (8 ounces); sesame oil (2 teaspoons); sesame seeds (1 teaspoon); garlic cloves, grated (2 pieces); watercress, trimmed, roughly chopped (1 bunch)

Instructions: 1) Pour the sesame oil into a skillet (nonstick) and heat on medium-low. Add the ginger and garlic and cook for 2 minutes. 2) Turn the heat up to medium before stirring in the mushrooms. Cook for another 4 minutes, then stir in the watercress. Cook for an additional 2 to 3 minutes. 3) Line a pan with foil, add the sesame seeds, and toast in a toaster oven. Add the seeds on top of the mushroom mixture.

Nice 'n' Easy Turkey Grilled Cheese

Ingredients: pesto (1 teaspoon); cheddar cheese, sliced (1 ounce); bread slices, sprouted grain (2 pieces); turkey, fresh, sliced (2 ounces); tomato slices, 1/8-inch (2 pieces)

Instructions: 1) Heat the grill pan before misting with cooking spray. 2) Cover one bread slice with the pesto. Top with the sliced cheese, turkey, and tomato before adding on the remaining bread slice. 3) Place the sandwich on the preheated pan and grill one each side for 1 to 2 minutes.

Meaty Mixed Veggie Stew

Ingredients: garlic, chopped (1/2 teaspoon); beef, grass-fed, ground (4 ounces); olive oil, extra virgin (1 teaspoon); assorted vegetables, chopped (2 cups); sweet potato, baked (1 piece)

Instructions: 1) Add oil to a saucepan heated on medium. Turn heat down to low before stirring in and cooking the garlic for 2 to 3 minutes. 2) Stir in the chopped vegetables and cook until softened. Stir in the ground meat and cook until browned through. 3) Serve alongside the baked sweet potato.

Scrumptious Lettuce Cups

Ingredients: lettuce heads (2 pieces); lemon dressing (2 tablespoons); tabbouleh salad (2 cups); rotisserie chicken, whole (1 piece); carrots, shredded (1/2 cup); red peppers, sliced thinly (1/2 cup); avocado, sliced (1 piece)

Instructions: 1) Remove the skin off the chicken, then shred the meat. 2) Add the lemon dressing to the shredded vegetables and toss to combine. 3) Fill the lettuce leaves with equal portions of the tabbouleh salad, dressed veggies, and shredded chicken.

8

MINIMALIST FITNESS HABITS

Fitness does not have to mean paying for an overpriced gym membership, supplements, gadgets like FitBits, and personal training packages — if you take up these minimalist fitness habits:

1. Perform exercise routines that you actually enjoy.

Do not waste your time on doing the things that you hate, so do not take up running if you cannot stand it. If you have decided that you detest all forms of exercise, give other workout routines a try. You might actually love yoga, walking, acrobatics, or Zumba.

2. Adopt lifestyle changes instead of constantly following the latest diet.

It can be hard to follow any strict diet if it sets rules that are too many and too complicated to remember. Forget about attempting to adopt fad diets that force you to remember the number of calories you could only consume in a day or the kinds of food you need to avoid. Change your lifestyle instead:

· Consume more vegetables, fruits, and other whole foods.

· Reduce your intake of processed foods.

· Make sure to eat only when you feel hungry.

· Get away from the table once you feel full.

3. Place more focus on health, less on appearance.

Focusing too much on how your body looks may keep you from feeling contented with your appearance, no matter how many hours you put into your workouts or how intensely you work on your routines. Know that someone else will always be stronger, leaner, or more physically attractive than you. When you concentrate on improving your image, you will feel de-motivated to exercise and ultimately believe that working out would be pointless. The best thing you can do is to focus on your health instead. Ponder upon everything that you are able to do at present that you would have thought unimaginable a few years, months, or weeks ago. It will help if you pay attention to how stronger your body is compared to before you took up exercising.

4. Purchase only the things you need.

Avoid wasting your money on expensive gym memberships and exercise-related gadgets, especially if you know you will not be using those things anyway. Getting in shape only requires you to wear comfortable clothes and to have a drinking water bottle. If you plan on working out at home, consider buying a yoga mat or a pair of handheld weights, both of which do not cost that much.

5. Begin by giving the following minimalist yoga workout ideas a try.

You will find that yoga sun salutations are ideal as your minimalist workout.

Performing them do not take up that much space, do not require you to purchase expensive apparatus, and encourage you to be mindful of how your body moves.

Try the following yoga poses at home:

· Stand with your heels slightly apart, making sure your big toes are touching and your feet's outer edges are parallel. Let your arms hang in a relaxed manner on your sides, with your palms held wide open.

· Breathe in as you raise your arms straight up, then take both palms together into a praying position over the head. Breathe out, then bring your hands' praying position down your body's middle section as you fold down to a bent-forward position.

· Breathe in, bringing your body into a long, flat spine as you touch the ground with your fingertips or as you place your hands on your shins. Breathe out, planting your palms on the ground (make sure they are shoulder-width apart), then jump up and hold your body in a position where your elbows are grazing your rib cage.

· Breathe out, then flip over your toes as you lift your hips while keeping your legs lengthened, before pressing your chest back between both arms. Have your heels reach toward the ground.

· Breathe in, bringing your body upward on the balls of your feet, softening your knees, and gazing between your hands. Breathe out, lifting your hips up before you jump up to your yoga mat's front. Breathe in as you bring your body again to a long and flat spine, then breathe out as you bend forward.

· Breathe in and hinge from your hips (with a long spine) in order to bring your body up to a standing position. Stretch your arms over your head into a high praying position, then exhale as you bring the same position down to the middle of your chest. Breathe in to complete the routine.

· Repeat the routine four more times.

9

MINIMALIST DRESSING HABITS

Practicing minimalist dressing habits means simplifying your wardrobe, which results in being able to open the closet and just pick out the pieces that help make you feel good, look good, and ready to conquer the day's tasks.

Here are tips to help you adopt a minimalist fashion style with less clothing items:

1. Accept the fact that you simply own too many clothes.

The reasons people own too many clothes can include aspiring for a future self or lifestyle (having a slimmer physique, going on a safari, attending a black-tie affair), imagining other people's envy over your new outfit, and visualizing how glamorous/young/cool you will look wearing your latest finds. In your case, it may be because you love several items in your wardrobe too much that you always put off wearing them for fear of ruining them, or you have a duplicate for every favorite blouse you own because you would hate it if you could no longer wear them. Just face up to the reality — you are wallowing in too many clothes.

2. Decide to inject fewer colors into your wardrobe.

Choose your favorite colors, which you often wear because you like the way you look and feel in them. This way, you also need to wear fewer accessories such as handbags, belts, shoes, and jewelry.

3. Make sure to keep only the clothes that fit your body.

Once you start paring down your wardrobe, take the time to see which garments still fit and which need to be repaired. This task can seem troublesome at first, but in order to have a minimalist wardrobe, you need to get rid of those garments that you hung onto because you believe you will get to wear them again once you lose/gain weight or once you have finally have them altered or repaired. If you have a quality dress that needs tweaking, ask yourself if you really need to have it tailored; if so, then take the dress to the tailor right away. (If the dress is still hanging in your closet after three days, you need to let it go.)

4. Know what to keep and what to toss.

You may have clothes in the closet that always make you feel special whenever you wear them — keep them. As for those items that make you feel and look so-so, as well as those that you bought on impulse, received as gifts but never got around to wearing, or no longer fit, feel free to let them go.

5. Choose good quality.

If there are certain clothing items that you need, make sure to buy those that are well-constructed and made with quality materials. Avoid purchasing any garment because it is discounted or part of a buy-one-take-one promo. Check how the clothes you are going to buy are sewn — inspect the stitching quality, fabric weight, fit, and drape. If you have to buy essentials like black trousers, you can give yourself some leeway and splurge on a bit more expensive but high quality pair. This tip also applies to any new purchase that you can easily mix and match with the items you already have in your closet, especially if it flatters your personality, lifestyle, shape, and size. Go for quality clothing that will look as good after many washings as the day you bought it.

6. Give the capsule wardrobe a try.

A capsule wardrobe is not about owning black, gray, or plain everything. Instead, it means ensuring that every item you have in your closet can be matched or layered with four or more other items. You could pair your navy cardigan with a beige skirt, a navy dress, and a number of plain or printed blouses. You could wear your favorite floral top with dark wash or light wash jeans, gray slacks, a black leather skirt, or under the navy cardigan.

7. Consider uniform dressing.

Adopting a uniform dressing style does not involve wearing a single outfit over and over again for an entire week. What it means is selecting a few key silhouettes or styles that flatter you and then watching for items that have a similar silhouette or style. Be on the lookout for items that you could layer easily, such as a knit shirt, a tank, a blazer, a cardigan, or a button-down. You can then pair these items with skinny jeans, straight-leg trousers, a midi skirt, or a pencil skirt. Once you figure out your uniform's basic components, it will be easier for you to think up more outfits by simply mixing and accessorizing them.

10

MINIMALIST SHOPPING HABITS

To shop the minimalist way is to pay more attention to the process and to be more deliberate with the items that you choose to purchase and add to your home. This way, you obtain only what you need or love, without adding clutter to your space and life. Here are 10 minimalist shopping habits you can adopt:

1. Give up the store email subscriptions.

An effective way of avoiding impulse buying and shopping minimally instead is eliminating as many temptations as possible. Retailers are experts at marketing their products, which includes sending you emails to inform you about their best sales ever. Resist the lure of buying on impulse anything that you have no need of by unsubscribing from these store emails. You will find it easier to make deliberate purchases if you are seeking out those items, instead of being assailed with sale offers on items you never thought about wanting at all.

2. Steer clear of shopping centers.

Another habit to adopt in the name of shopping like a minimalist is to get yourself as far away as possible from shopping centers or malls. Spending plenty of time in these places puts you right where retailers can effectively bombard you with advertisements until you break down and forget about your decision to stop buying more and owning more things you do not need or love. Replace your mall trips with other hobbies, particularly those that do not involve shopping.

3. Be prepared to shop.

Make sure to do your research prior to buying something. Checking out online reviews would be helpful, as these reviews let you weigh the advantages and disadvantages of purchasing an item. When you research your buying options first, you avoid being tempted by the idea of simply having something new to call your own; rather, you are giving yourself the opportunity to decide if you really need or love that item and that it meets your expectations.

Once you are done researching your would-be purchases, allow yourself some time to think things through (including the reasons you want to buy the items), then create a list of all the items you are intentionally buying. See to it that you stick to that list to keep yourself from buying anything on a whim.

4. Mull it over.

It is too easy to become so excited over the prospect of purchasing something new that it is also too easy to forget about the regret that comes later. Avoid such circumstances by waiting for as long as 24 hours before heading for the store. Doing so gives you the time you need to mull over your planned purchase and increases your chances of avoiding the impulse purchase trap.

5. Mull it over some more.

Write down that thing you are planning to buy and then wait for 30 days. Once your month of mulling is over, decide whether or not you are still considering the idea of making that purchase. You may be surprised to find that, after all that time you spent thinking about your planned purchase, you do not really need or want that item after all.

6. Use cash to pay for everything.

Use cash when buying something instead of your credit card or debit card. This way, you are forcing yourself to spend less money — it does hurt more when you pay with the cash you now have than if you gradually paid over time with the money you are hoping to have sooner or later.

7. Buy something new only after wearing out what you already have.

Never buy anything new if the one you already own is not yet worn out or used up. Doing so helps you avid owning duplicates that only clutter up your space.

8. Plan to spend nothing.

Set aside a day, week, or month for spending absolutely nothing. Imposing a spending freeze on yourself can effectively help you determine the shopping habits you need to eliminate from your lifestyle, as well as identify the areas in your life where you could cut down on your expenses.

9. Examine your purpose for purchasing something.

Prior to making your purchase, make sure to ask yourself why you really want to buy that particular thing. Could your reason be that, after much consideration, you believe it will bring significance to your life? Or maybe it's because you find your current belongings boring and you have to have something new to own? Could it be that having that particular item will make you feel you have "arrived"? Or it might be because you simply need to impress your co-worker or neighbor? Many times, people end up buying stuff for one wrong reason or another. Start shopping minimally by being clear about your purpose for buying something.

10. Choose to spend on experiences rather than material things.

Instead of buying a gift (book, wallet, or belt) for your friend, give him/her something that is consumable and unlikely to clutter up his/her space, such as tickets to his/her favorite concert, guitar lesson fees, passes to a local museum, or dinner-out gift cards. When buying yourself a gift, forego that perfume or purse and go instead for a spa, a movie, a coffee date with friends, or a yoga class.

11

DIGITAL MINIMALISM HABITS

Digital minimalism refers to ridding your digital life of the excesses in order to have and use only what is essential in a most efficient manner. Being a minimalist in your digital life means questioning the value that a piece of technology (including your phone, Internet, email, and social media) adds to your life.

Apply these digital minimalism habits for a more simplified, efficient online life:

1. Do your digital simplifying in baby steps.

There are some individuals who feel helpless if a few minutes go by without having checked their emails or smartphone. There are also plenty of others who have made it a habit or reflex to constantly check for social media updates. If you find yourself belonging to these groups of individuals, you may need to take small steps in taking a minimalist approach to your digital life. It would be helpful to think that you are teaching yourself to go on a digital diet. Begin by challenging yourself to go for 15 minutes without looking at or thinking about any form of technology. Next, gradually increase the periods in which you avoid logging into Facebook, Gmail, and Twitter. Do this in manageable increments: Start with half an hour, then build up to one hour, then to two hours, until it becomes a habit for you to go for several hours without having to be online.

2. Establish daily periods of shunning screen time.

Every day, set aside periods of keeping yourself away from technology, which is one effective way of reducing your need for technology to acceptable levels. You can start by imposing on yourself non-screen times during breakfast, lunch, dinner, and bedtime. It also helps to keep the rooms where you eat and sleep free from any forms of digital device. Other tricks you can apply to yourself is to avoid checking your emails between 6 to 8 in the evening or whenever you are cooking and then sitting down to dinner with your family; doing without the Internet for an entire Saturday; being content with watching TV on weekends; refusing to scroll through or even look at your smartphone when having lunch at work; and never bringing your tablet or cell phone to the dinner table.

3. Set aside a schedule for answering emails.

Make sure to reply to texts and emails only during scheduled times, although you may make exceptions for messages coming from select individuals that you have on call (assuming that any message you receive from them means an emergency). Checking your emails only 3 times a day will provide you plenty of saved time, so impose a rule that you can only view your inbox at 9 a.m., 1 p.m., and 4 p.m. Make the decision to turn off your social media and email in order to resist the temptation to always check your mobile devices; it also helps to disable those push notifications and to set your devices to silent mode at certain times of the day. Lastly, avoid using your cellphone as a handy alarm clock.

4. Take pleasure in non-technology entertainment.

You will automatically reduce your screen time if you engage in activities that are incompatible with digital use, such as meditating, jogging, walking outdoors, or swimming. It also helps to go to a yoga class, a place of worship, or other places that do not allow the use of technology. You might also:

· Make a game out of people's habit of constantly checking their phones in social situations. For example, if you are in a pub, you could challenge your friends to a game where the first person to check his or her phone will have to buy everyone their preferred drinks.

· Allow yourself to enjoy the silence that comes with staying out of touch with technology for a certain amount of time. Take time to go to places where you could just sit back and quietly contemplate minus any technological distractions.

· Resolve to be productive without any help from technology: Catch up on your reading, write in your journal, or finish your cross-stitch/jewelry-making/acrylic painting project.

5. Trim down your list of contacts.

It is easier to practice digital minimalism when you shrink the number of your social media friends, followed blogs, used apps, and online group subscriptions. Rid your phone of all social media apps you do not use that much. For the remaining apps, reset the passwords to hard-to-remember ones. Unfollow blogs you don't read anyway. Lastly, go over your list of contacts, then delete those numbers you no longer need.

12

SIMPLIFIED MONEY MANAGEMENT HABITS

Adopting simplified money management habits will help you declutter your finances, give priority to your most pressing financial goals, and live the minimalist lifestyle without worrying how you are going to pay next month's bills. The minimalist way of managing your finances does not mean figuring out how to save the most dollars; rather, it is about establishing an easier system to help you meet your daily needs and reach your goals with peace of mind.

1. Commit to owning instead of borrowing.

This may sound contradictory to what minimalism extols (own less, spend less), but it actually means changing your mindset about the use of your money. You are better off spending your hard-earned money in owning something instead of using it to pay off a loan you applied for in order to get the very same thing you could have just paid for outright in the first place.

You have probably heard of people getting broke as a result of owning stuff by way of loan payments. You may hear a financially challenged friend talk about buying a car after learning he/she only had to pay 200 dollars a month for it. You can see where your friend made a financial mistake — the goal was to stretch out financial resources as much as possible. By seeing to it that he/she makes the lowest payments, your friend believes he/she is free to live beyond his/her means, in the kind of lifestyle that he/she aspires for but could not really afford.

But by deciding to own things through purchasing rather than borrowing, you will no longer think of your stuff in terms of how many payments are left until you can truly call them "your" stuff. The best thing you can do when you need to have something is to buy it right away, not to ask how much the monthly payments would be.

2. Seriously consider paying yourself first.

Making this a habit will greatly help in ensuring that you always have something to fall back on when money is hard to come by. Opt to automatically pay yourself ahead of everything else by setting up with your bank an automatic transfer from a checking account to a savings account. As an alternative, you might also try setting up reoccurring direct deposits into your savings account; that way, you never have to actually see your money, which frees you from the dilemma of deciding whether to save it or spend it. You know you will never lack for things to blow your hard-earned cash on, so eliminate that decision by having your savings automated.

3. Create a minimalist budget.

· Collect all of your financial statements, including your recent utility bills, bank statements, and investment accounts.

· Log all your financial resources or income sources. If you do odd jobs on the side or are self-employed, make sure to include those data in your record. If you earn your income through regular paychecks (after automatic deduction of taxes), you can record your take-home pay or net income. You can then write down the total of your income in the form of a monthly amount.

• Make a record of all of your monthly expenses. List all your expected expenses in a month, including your utilities, groceries, car payments, mortgage payments, student loans, auto insurance, college savings, retirement savings, dry cleaning, and entertainment.

• Categorize your expenses into fixed and variable expenses. Your fixed expenses include those you need to pay each month in relatively fixed amounts and are essential for daily living, such as your rent/mortgage, credit card payments, car payments, Internet/cable service, and even trash pickup. Meanwhile, your variable expenses are the ones for which you will be paying in different amounts each month, such as your groceries, gifts, gasoline, eating out, and entertainment.

• Get the sum of all your monthly expenses as well as monthly income. In case the figure you end up with shows that your income is greater than your expenses, consider yourself on the right track — you have the advantage of prioritizing your extra income to more pressing areas of the budget you are working with, such as your credit card balances, retirement fund, and debts. On the other hand, you need to make changes in your budget if you end up with a greater total for your expenses than your income.

• Make those necessary changes to your expenses. After checking that you have made an accurate list of all your expenses, your final objective should be ensuring that your income column equals your expense column. To achieve this, you have to make sure all your sources of income are accounted for and put toward a specific savings goal or expense. If you find yourself having more expenses than your income can afford, the best thing to do would be to look for ways in which you could cut back on your variable expenses. This should be easy, as your variable expenses are usually those in the non-essentials category (think weekly dinners at the restaurant or monthly gym membership fees).

• Go over your budget on a monthly basis. Reviewing your budget every month is important, as this is the best way for you to stay on top of your finances. It helps to sit down after the first month and make a comparison of your actual expenses and the ones you included in your budget. Doing so helps you determine where you are doing well and where you will have to make some improvements.

4. Allot less for spending.

As soon as you come up with a budget that works for your minimalist lifestyle, income, and expenses, you have to decide to reduce the amount of money to use on spending. This will enable you to have extra money to use in paying off your existing debts as well as building your emergency fund. Once you are able to pay off those debts, you will end up with more money to allot for spending every month. In the beginning, you will find that your challenge is to search for ways you could save in almost all categories of your expenses. In time, your saving savvy will improve and you will find it easier to save on food costs, family vacations, and movies.

An important tip for reducing your expenses is to dare yourself to slash 50 dollars a week from your groceries. You will find that cutting back on your spending in increments makes the whole thing easier to manage and makes you more likely to succeed. Rather than fully eliminating one category from your expenses, you may be better off reducing the amount you spend in all categories by 10 to 20 dollars per month. Your extra savings will grow at a faster rate this way, and you can always challenge yourself to slash off bigger amounts the following month.

5. Put away a certain amount each month.

Having money put away in the bank is easy if you make sure to take a certain amount from your paycheck each month. To build your preliminary emergency fund, strive to have one month's worth of salary in your bank account.

Then, when you are finally done with your debts, you can start establishing a bigger emergency fund. You might try taking 10 to 20 percent from your monthly paycheck and add it to your emergency fund. Once you have yourself an amount that equals your expenses for an entire year, you will find yourself feeling more prepared to handle unforeseen circumstances that would have meant financial disasters if you did not have an emergency fund put away. Starting at a mere 50 dollars per paycheck will help improve your financial confidence.

The key here is to avoid dipping into your emergency fund as soon as you start putting it away. If you find yourself becoming tempted to touch your savings, take steps to make it difficult for you to do so. You could open a separate savings account in another bank or online. You will certainly find your impulse to spend abruptly curbed by the thought of taking that extra trip to the other bank or waiting for 2 to 3 days before you could access your savings. It also helps to try placing a small part of your savings in a 3-month certificate of deposit so that you cannot touch the money at all.

6. Never depend on bonuses for getting by in your finances.

If the company you work for offers bonuses on a regular basis, you may start relying on those bonuses and include them in your budget. This is a wrong move, since bonuses are not guaranteed sources of income – your company could, at any point, stop handing out those bonuses, shutting down your dreams of making ends meet. What you should do instead is to make a separate spending plan that is specifically just for your bonuses. It would be a great idea to use the windfalls in quickly paying off your outstanding debts or growing your emergency fund.

7. Remove your debts from your life.

• Discard your credit cards. You cannot expect to get yourself out of debt if you keep putting money on a credit card (or two or more). You have to decide to stop your credit card use until you've gotten rid of your debt, even if you think the rewards they provide make your credit cards worth their while. Doing so will effectively improve your spending. If you do not have the guts to do that, try cutting up every single credit card you own. Or save just one credit card, which is where you will place all your credit, making sure to pay off the amount you incur on it every month.

• Until you are not done paying off your debts, it helps to keep yourself from taking out loans of any kind. You could stop relying on your credit cards to ease yourself out of a financial situation, like an unexpected car repair, since you have your emergency fund to help you pay for it. If your desire is to pay off your debt faster, consider taking on a part-time job. The income you derive from it will then go toward those debts. Then, once your debts are cleared, you can decide to stop moonlighting and rest assured that your financial situation has now improved.

• Determine which debts need to be paid off first. This usually means your credit card debts, since they carry higher interest rates compared to other types of debts. Decide which among your credit cards deserve to be repaid first — it should be the one costing you the most money because it is also the one having the highest interest rate. Look at your list of debts and rank each item to figure out the order you will be paying them off.

• Draw up a monthly payment calendar for your bills. This will help you identify the specific bills you need to pay with a specific source of income or paycheck. Write on the calendar the payment amount required by each bill beside its due date; you could then fill in each paycheck's date. If you typically receive your paychecks on the same day each month, you can use one monthly payment calendar every month. However, if you receive your paychecks on different days, then you are better off drawing up a new calendar every month.

· Look for ways you could resist the temptation to spend impulsively. Try tweaking your budget so that you can only buy stuff with cash. Or prepare an envelope for each expense, with each envelope containing only a certain amount of cash — tough if an envelope gets emptied out before your next paycheck. Switching to cash helps you curb your impulse spending tendencies since it is glaringly obvious when there is no more cash to spare. To make this strategy truly work, never run to your credit cards or debit cards once you have reached your cash limit. When heading to the mall, make sure to leave those credit cards safely tucked under the bed.

· Quit taking in more debts. Although doing so does not single-handedly help resolve your debts, it does prevent them from getting worse. If you keep creating additional debt while you are making payments on it, you can hardly make progress, if at all. Avoid being tempted to create additional debts by having your credit frozen and cutting up all your credit cards.

· Increase the amount you pay monthly. You will have a difficult time getting yourself out of debt if you are just paying the minimum on those debts. You will find yourself having paid two or three times the original amount by the time your balance is fully paid off with minimum payments. The only time it is all right to pay off credit card charges with minimum payments is when you are following a debt-repayment mechanism wherein you need to pay a large amount on one of the credit cards you own.

· Set up an emergency fund. You may think this idea sounds off, given that since you are attempting to get yourself out of debt, you should be putting that money on your debts instead of putting it in a new savings account. But then having an emergency fund actually prevents you from creating additional debts — if an emergency comes up, you can dip into your emergency fund instead of using your credit card again. You can build up a minimum of 1,000 dollars in the beginning, then work your way up to 6 to 12 months' worth of your living expenses.

• Select one debt which you will focus on. While there is merit in increasing all your payments by a small amount, doing so means the payments you make on them only get reduced a little every month. By committing to making a large payment on one of your debts every month until it is fully paid off, you will certainly make more tangible progress. Meanwhile, you can continue making the minimum payments on the rest of your accounts. Then make a large payment each month on another account, and then another account, until all of your debts are completely repaid.

• Request for a reduced interest rate from your creditor. Trying to pay off your debt with higher interest rates actually keeps you longer in debt because a big chunk of what you are paying goes to those interest charges instead of your actual balance. Negotiate with your creditor so you can have your interest rate lowered, which should go well if you made sure to have a good payment history. If you decide to obtain a lower interest rate by using a balance transfer, make sure you pay off your balance prior to the expiration of the promotional rate; afterward, your balance goes back to being subjected to a higher interest rate.

13

WORK MINIMALISM HABITS

Applying the principles of minimalism to your work habits will help you tackle your commitments and goals more effectively as well as produce more results with considerably less input. Rather than forcing yourself to have more output by cramming too many menial tasks into your schedule, practicing minimalist work habits enables you to set aside more time for doing other important things.

Let the following tips help you apply minimalism toward work:

1. Begin by making sure you have a clean workspace to work with.

You may have heard of other people who believe that messiness is actually a sign of one's genius. But know that a cluttered work area can cause you to focus less on your tasks as well as waste too much time trying to accomplish them.

2. Reduce the number of items on your list of to-dos.

It is not hard to feel discouraged and stressed when you have to deal with a lengthy list of tasks that are not finished yet. Take advantage of minimalism's power by attacking your to-dos with a whiteout or eraser. See to it that your daily list of tasks contains just up to three items.

3. Write everything down.

Writing down every single task you need to do is a way of doing a "mind dump." It involves allotting half an hour to jotting down all the activities you need to tackle and any worries that may be bugging you. Once you have "dumped" everything from your mind, simply set aside your list and then cross the thing off your mind. This exercise helps you stop your mental list of things-to-do from following you around, causing you to lose focus on the task at hand.

4. Know how to say no.

Living the minimalist lifestyle involves learning one of the key elements of increasing your productivity while doing less, which is saying no to tasks that do not add to your life's value — other people's requests that may be urgent but are not part of your responsibilities, meetings that you know are unnecessary, and social obligations that you would rather not fulfill. As long as you are unable to beg off doing any of those things, you will never have the time and energy for focusing on things that matter most to you, and your productivity decreases. Effectively decline a request by saying no in a polite but firm manner, making sure you do not sound as though you are stalling. It also helps to replace your "I can't" answers with "I don't," since this gives you a sense of being in control of the situation as well as leaves no room for negotiation or debate.

5. Avoid multitasking.

It may appear that you will be able to perform your tasks with greater efficiency by multitasking, but studies have indicated that this work habit actually reduces productivity by as much as 40 percent. Not only is your productivity hindered by multitasking, your creativity is also reduced. Quit the habit of multitasking by setting aside a chunk of your time for working on a single task. Turn off your phone, avoid checking your social media updates, give your Internet browser a rest, and leave your email inbox alone.

6. Have a break.

Take the time to have a meaningful break instead of giving in to the temptation of working through lunch and bringing your work home. Research has identified the power of taking meaningful breaks to reduce stress and increase productivity. When you fail to take regular breaks, your ability to focus on things dramatically drops, which is why it is recommended by experts that people intentionally walk away from their workspace every 60 to 90 minutes, and then spend 3 to 5 minutes getting water to drink, fixing a snack, chatting with co-workers, or simply stretching their limbs. Make sure to use a different space for each activity, which means you should never try eating lunch on your computer desk.

14

MINIMALIST TRAVELING HABITS

The minimalist lifestyle does not only involve decluttering your home, your wardrobe, and your finances. Minimalism is also about traveling and seeing the world in an empowering way, particularly if the trip you are planning will be a long one and you are on a tight budget. Know that wanting to accumulate possessions can hinder you from going on spontaneous traveling experiences as well as fully being "there" during the exciting moments of your explorations. When you travel minimally, you will be able to take advantage of less expensive flight fares, experience more comfort on the road, reduce your chances of being robbed, reduce the time wasted on waiting for your bags to turn up, and have a blast getting yourself immersed in local cultures.

Several tweaks are all that is needed to help you take on the minimalist way of traveling to new places. Follow the tips below on how to pack, plan, and take a trip the way a minimalist does:

1. Get yourself a bag that's well-organized.

Minimalism does teach you to give up buying lots of stuff to fill a void in your life, but it would actually be best for a devoted traveler like you to invest in a quality, well-organized bag that you can use for a long period of time. You will do great choosing an ergonomic one, especially if it comes with lots of pockets for more versatility (pockets enable you to keep your clothes, toiletries, and electronics separate and organized). Go for a backpack you could depend on to easily transform itself into a rolled suitcase and that comes with a daypack that can be conveniently detached.

2. Go over your toiletries bag with a critical eye.

Toiletries are notorious for taking up plenty of space inside a suitcase, and they also tend to burst under pressure, making them prone to leaking and creating a huge mess. Traveling minimally means leaving your 37 beauty devices and 11 restorative elixirs behind and focusing instead on bringing along just the basics for good grooming — think soap, deodorant, toothpaste, toothbrush, lotion, and shampoo. If you find that you will be needing a bug repellant spray and sunscreen during the trip, you could always just pick them up along the way.

3. Take along only the clothes you will need to wear.

When going the minimalist traveling route, it would be helpful if you leave your fashionista identity at home and embrace a more minimalist approach to dressing yourself up. Rather than packing your bag with the OOTDs you have in mind, pare the garments you will bring on the trip down to the ones you absolutely need. Remember that clothes made of wool are your travel buddies, as they dry fast, insulate you well, do not wrinkle easily, and are naturally odor-resistant. It also helps to make sure to tightly roll your garments before placing them inside your bag, since doing so conserves space and minimizes the chances of their being wrinkled.

4. Accept the fact that you will have to do laundry.

This is especially unavoidable if you are planning to travel for more than a week. You cannot call it minimalist traveling if you will be bringing 10 different outfits for your 10-day vacation. Traveling minimally is a good time to take advantage of laundromats in towns and cities. Do your on-the-road laundry with minimal to no fuss with the help of change machines and detergent dispensers available in these laundromats. Take your minimalist approach to traveling a notch higher by washing your worn clothes in the tub or sink where you are staying.

5. Wear your natural skin and hair with pride.

Traveling minimally is the best time to love the skin and hair you were born with (except when the reason you are traveling is to attend a special event that requires you to present your best-looking self). Minimalist traveling also lets you enjoy the freedom of letting your makeup-free face breathe and your product-free hair take a break from all the gunk you usually style it with. You will survive your trip even if you leave your foundation, bronzer, mascara, curling iron, and hair dryer at home.

6. Wear your most comfortable and versatile footwear.

There is nothing minimalist about packing on a single pair of the latest "It" shoes if they are only going to give you discomfort and blisters during the trip. Expect to do lots of walking while you are traveling, which is why it would be wise to wear your most comfortable shoes. Choose one that will go with every outfit you are bringing along for the trip and would fit right in where you are going.

7. Bring along a tablet or an eReader instead of a book.

Traveling is often the best time for catching up on your reading, such as while you are riding a bus, waiting for your order at a café, and before tucking yourself into bed after a day of sightseeing and even people-watching. Forget about bringing along your favorite heavy book or two and take instead an eReader, where all of the materials you will read are stored. You can also take your minimalist travel an extra mile further by downloading a reading app in your phone.

8. Take a minimalist approach when deciding which electronic devices to bring.

You will find that your smartphone may be all that you need during the trip, as it does enable you to stay in touch with family and friends and to take lots of pictures of the sights you will be visiting, as well as help you with directions and safety. You would be better off leaving your laptop and other office electronics at home — seriously, will you possibly have the time and energy to work while traveling? It goes without saying that not lugging your heavy devices during the trip means you are also free from bringing along their tangled cords and wires.

9. Purchase groceries.

If you are traveling minimally on a budget, purchasing groceries would be a sensible idea. Go to the nearest local grocery store to shop for ingredients, then cook your meals in hotels or hostels with kitchens. You could even prepare extras to store inside resealable bags or plastic storage containers, which you could then snack on or eat as a meal later. If the place you are going to is known to have safe water to drink, you can simply take a refillable water bottle to help you stay well-hydrated during your entire trip. Doing so actually helps you not only to reduce the clutter generated during your trip, but also reduce the waste you create in the environment.

10. Plan on shipping back your souvenirs.

Souvenir shopping may be considered as one of the most looked-forward-to part of any trip for most people. A minimalist like you can still buy souvenirs, but instead of buying big, heavy ones, choose ornaments, jewelry, patches, magnets, and other easily portable items. You could then have them shipped back home to avoid having to carry them and worrying they might break on the trip back.

15

MIND DECLUTTERING HABITS

Your mind also needs some tidying up from mental clutter every once in a while. It is hard to live a minimalist life when your mind is constantly bogged down by mental baggage, so declutter it with the help of these tips:

1. Maintain a gratitude notebook.

To practice gratitude means to appreciate the things that you have in your life and accepting that such things are enough. You will find more balance in your life if you just take time each day to be thankful for your blessings. Also, remember that being grateful makes it harder to be angry. So make sure to take 5 minutes off each day to write down at least 5 things you are grateful for in your life. These could include times spent with your family and friends, a recognition your child received in school, the clean air in your neighborhood, your clear eyesight, your wonderful relationship with your partner, or the soothing sounds of raindrops falling on the roof.

2. Take the time to just laugh your head off.

Everyone probably knows about the power of laughter to relieve stress. Laughter melts away feelings of defensiveness and bad emotions as well as helps you enjoy being in the moment. Try laughing more often and avoid taking yourself too seriously. Go for a really deep and hearty laugh, which comes easily when you are hanging out with a friend who has the knack for jokes, watching comedies, playing with your kids or pets, and reading Archie comics.

3. Unplug from media.

It will not do your mind any good if you end up listening to or watching any show that you come across. The subtle messages, judgments, and biases they send make their way into your mind and end up cluttering it with mental garbage. You could find yourself forming opinions that are simply based on what you heard or saw. This is the reason limiting your exposure to media is beneficial to your minimalist well-being.

Here are several tips to help you in media fasting:

· A media fast does not involve retreating to the mountains for a month and foregoing TV, electricity, and running water. You could simply designate one hour per night as your media-fasting period, have a lively talk with your family over dinner, and then take a walk with your dog. If you would rather have a longer media fast, try doing it on weekends to avoid worrying about work. And if you are daring enough and have the resources and time for a lengthy break, consider going on a seven-day camping trip.

· You could start your media fast by limiting yourself to one form of media per day, especially if it is something you need to use for work reasons. Although this strategy is not as hardcore as a total media fast, it is still much better than nothing.

· Know that your media fast journey is not something you have to do all on your own. While the act of fasting is typically believed to be a solitary experience, you can actually encourage your family and friends to join you in media fasting so that they could also enjoy its main benefit, which is forming deeper connections with other people. Consider organizing Monopoly games at home or a friendly soccer tournament at the local park, making sure everybody leaves their phones and gadgets alone. You might also suggest spending a quiet evening engaging in pleasant conversation, free from the distractions of TV noises or the glare from the computer screen.

· Accept the fact that doing a media fast is hardly within your comfort zone. You may feel your fingers beginning to twitch as it longs for the sensation of swiping across your tablet or smartphone. You may also experience feelings of isolation and anxiety due to being so out of touch with what is going on in social media. You may also find yourself facing moments of boredom head-on, which you used to temporarily forget by scrolling down your phone. That's okay. Assure yourself that it's normal, and that you will get used to it.

4. Engage in regular physical activity.

Exercising on a regular basis provides you more energy, improves your mood, encourages better sleep, increases your focus, and helps you feel more positive and relaxed about yourself and your life in general. Regular exercise is also considered an effective medicine for a number of common emotional and mental health issues, as it lets an individual deal with problems in a healthy manner instead of relying on drugs or alcohol that only worsens his/her symptoms. Moreover, exercising regularly provides a great boost to the immune system as well as makes you less likely to feel the effects of stress.

Performing any type of exercise — really, all that is required is that you move your body — is good. But remember that you will reap bigger health benefits from exercise if you focus your mind on it rather than mindlessly going through the motions. It is important that you immerse yourself in that moment when your feet hit the pavement, when the wind touches your skin, or when you are taking deep breaths. Concentrating on how your entire body feels as you work out helps to not just improve your physical health, but also helps put a stop to any worrisome thoughts that constantly run through your mind.

There is no need for you to put in 2 to 3 hours a day sweating it out at the gym or running mile after mile in order to reap exercise's health benefits. Thirty minutes worth of moderate physical activity is okay, as long as you make sure to do it 5 times per week. If your schedule does not permit you to work out that often, you could always break a 30-minute-long session into 3 10-minute sessions, which are spread out throughout the day.

5. Stop worrying.

Worrying gets you nowhere, so let go of those negative feelings and anxious thoughts. Doing so regularly will help effectively reduce the mental clutter that robs you of energy and focus, both of which are better spent on more important things. Do away with worrying with these tricks:

· If you catch yourself worrying over something, step back for a minute and go over the things that you can control. You know there is nothing you could do to keep a storm from brewing, but you can certainly take measures in preparing for it. There is no way you could prevent someone from behaving in a particular way, but you have full control of your reaction to such behavior. It helps to realize that there are times when the only things that you could be in charge of are your attitude and your effort. You will find yourself becoming more effective in everything you do once you focus your energy on those things you have power over.

· Let go of worrying for some time. There are times when the only thing you could do about worrying is to postpone doing so. Consider putting off those anxieties at a later time if worrying prevents you from accomplishing your daily tasks. You may allow yourself to worry, but make sure to do it only during a certain time.

· Write down the things you are worrying about. Doing so actually helps you feel that you can manage your problems.

· Talk to someone about the things that cause you to worry. When you share your worries to others, you will learn to look at your sources of worry at another angle, which helps put things in the right perspective and lead you right to the root of all your troubles.

· Make sure you do not have lots of idle time on your hands. It truly helps to keep yourself busy in order to avoid worrying yourself to death. You will find yourself feeling less worried and stressed when you do some knitting, crafts, or other things you could do with your two hands. Studies have even shown that people who keep their hands busy while experiencing hurdles in life feel that their problems do not bother them as much.

· Consider aromatherapy. Using essential oils lets you achieve clarity, feel less worried and stressed, and experience an overall sense of well-being. You could mist your pillows with a few drops of lavender oil before tucking yourself into bed, freshen the ambience in your living room by lightly spraying the air with lemon oil, place orange oil-saturated cotton balls underneath the trash bin in the kitchen, and put several drops of chamomile oil on a toilet paper roll in your bathroom.

Conclusion

Thank you again for downloading this book!

I hope this book was able to help you to realize how holding on to your possessions have been holding you back from truly living your life and experiencing happiness and contentment.

The next step is to commit to applying the minimalism habits you learned from this book on a regular basis. Decide to make staying organized, purchasing purposefully, putting things back where they belong, focusing on your tasks, and kicking up your heels when it is time to relax part of your routine.

Thank you and good luck!

Thank You

Finally, if you enjoyed this book, then I'd like to ask you for a favor. Would you be kind enough to leave a review for this book ? It'd be greatly appreciated!

Thank you and good luck!

Copyright

of the trademark is without permission or backing by the trademark owner. All trademarks and brands within this book are for clarifying purposes only and are the owned by the owners themselves, not affiliated with this document.